Robert Shufflebotham

InDesign

COVERS CS3, CS4 & CS5

in
easy steps

For Windows and Mac

In easy steps is an imprint of In Easy Steps Limited
Southfield Road · Southam
Warwickshire CV47 0FB · United Kingdom
www.ineasysteps.com

Notice of Liability
Every effort has been made to ensure that this book contains accurate
and current information. However, In Easy Steps Limited and the
author shall not be liable for any loss or damage suffered by readers
as a result of any information contained herein.

Trademarks
Adobe® and InDesign® are registered trademarks of Adobe Systems
Incorporated. All other trademarks are acknowledged as belonging to
their respective companies.

In Easy Steps Limited supports The Forest Stewardship Council (FSC),
the leading international forest certification organisation. All our titles
that are printed on Greenpeace approved FSC certified paper carry the
FSC logo.

MIX
Paper from
responsible sources
FSC® C020837

Printed and bound in the United Kingdom

ISBN 978-1-84078-414-5

Contents

1 The Working Environment

This chapter takes a look at the working environment and gets you started using Adobe InDesign. It covers setting up a new document and introduces tool and panel conventions along with other useful techniques that will help make you accurate and productive as you start to use the software.

Learning InDesign

This book offers a unique approach to learning InDesign. Its prime purpose is to focus on the fundamental principles and core processes, common to all versions, that you need to know as you start using InDesign in order to become a confident, proficient and productive user. Master theses fundamentals and you can progress to exploit the full creative potential of a software application that is undoubtedly one of the most powerful, creative tools available.

Because of this clear focus and an approach that breaks down the software into easily digested learning sequences you can use this book to comfortably learn to use all recent versions of the software.

Importantly, *InDesign in easy steps* does not seek to cover every single function in InDesign. Such attempts can lead to information overload in the new user – all too often it's not quite clear what is essential and what is of marginal use, and as a result, the new user cannot develop a clear, logical learning strategy for understanding and then mastering new software.

Screenshots and versions

The screenshots used to illustrate the main steps on each page are taken from version CS5 of the software, from both the PC and Mac environments. In a high proportion of instances, the screenshots used are consistent in CS3, CS4 and CS5. Where necessary, screen shots from previous versions are included to illustrate changes and variations between versions.

Step by step instructions

Since the release of InDesign CS, the core functionality of InDesign has remained largely consistent and, based on considerable past experience, is likely to remain so for the next release of the software.

You can use this book with confidence to learn all recent versions of InDesign. Only one chapter – Chapter 17, Interactive – covers features available only in CS5.

Throughout the book the step by step instructions apply to all recent versions of the software, unless indicated otherwise, with explanatory notes, in either the text or in the version alert panels in the sidebar, where there are variations between versions of the software.

Enjoy learning.

The author

Robert Shufflebotham, a qualified teacher, has over 21 years of software training skill and experience.

He has trained and written In Easy Steps guides on InDesign since version 1 of the software. During this time he has developed a unique understanding of what it takes to get the best out of InDesign from the start.

Benefit from his considerable and varied experience distilled in the pages of this book as he guides you through the essential functionality that puts you on a course to successful mastery of the software.

Version Alerts

Watch out for version alerts in panels like this one. Where significant differences exist between different versions of the software they are highlighted and explained in these green panels.

The Tool Panel CS3 – CS5

To get a feel for how interface detail and functionality has evolved in InDesign versions from CS3 to CS5, take a look at the screen shots for each version of the Tool panel.

You'll see that some changes are largely cosmetic. For example, in CS3 the look and feel of the Tool panel changed from earlier versions and the toggle appearance button (▶▶) at the top of the panel was introduced, allowing you to easily change its appearance from single column to double column.

Sometimes new tools get added with a new version. For example, the Page tool and the Gap tool are new in CS5.

Occasionally, a tool is removed, for example, the Button tool introduced in version CS2 is no longer available in CS4 as different commands were introduced for creating multimedia style buttons.

But, even a fairly cursory look at the screenshots should convince you that there is considerable continuity in the toolset on offer across versions.

CS3   CS4   CS5

The Note tool appears for the first time in InDesign CS3.

The Gradient Feather tool makes its appearance in CS4 (see page 214 for further information) although you can create identical results using the Effects panel in CS3.

The Button tool disappears in CS4 making way for other techniques for creating interactive buttons.

The Position tool no longer appears in CS5 as the Content Grabber (see page 91) provides the same controls.

The Page tool (see page 30) and the Gap tool (see page 48) are introduced in InDesign CS5.

The Rotate, Scale and Shear tools become part of the Free Transform tool group in CS5.

Document Setup

Launch Adobe InDesign as you would any other application (from the Start menu – Windows, or from the Applications folder or Dock – Mac). When the InDesign splash screen and workspace appear you can create a new document.

Size and Orientation

1. To create a new document, choose File>New. The New Document dialog box appears. Use the Page Size drop-down list to choose a standard page size, if appropriate.

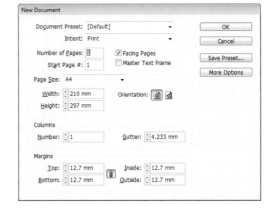

2. Select Master Text Frame to automatically create a text frame on the A-master that fits to the margins and matches the number of columns and gutter specified in the dialog box (see Chapter 10 for information in Master Pages).

3. Enter the number of pages you want in the document. If you are unsure of the number of pages you need, you can always add or delete pages when you are working in the document.

4. Choose the Facing Pages option to create a publication such as a magazine, brochure or book which will consist of double-page spreads. If you choose Facing Pages, Left and Right in the Margins area change to Inside and Outside, allowing you to set a wider inside margin to accommodate any binding edge in your document.

5. Use the Start Page # entry field if you want to start a document with a left hand page (in which case you enter an even number), or if you want to create a section as you set up a document. For example, if you enter an even number, InDesign creates a left hand page to begin the document, instead of the default right hand page. If you subsequently set up automatic page numbering (see page 145 for further details) the pages start numbering from the value you enter in this field.

6 To create a non-standard page size, make sure the Width entry field is highlighted, and then enter the page width you require. Then, do the same with the Height entry field.

7 Click the Landscape icon if you want to create a landscape page orientation. Portrait is selected by default.

Orientation:

Margin Guides

Set margin guides to define the main text area of your document. Margin guides are non-printing and appear as magenta lines on the screen. Margin guides are only guides – objects can be placed across margin guides or completely outside the margin guides.

1 Either enter values for Top, Bottom, Left/Right, Inside/ Outside.

2 Or click the "Make all settings the same" button ( ) to make it active, and then enter a value in one of the Margin entry fields. Press the Tab key to make all values the same as the first value you enter.

Column Guides

Column guides are non-printing and appear on screen as purple lines. They serve as a grid for constructing a publication. You are not constrained to working within the columns – all InDesign objects can cross column guides as necessary to create the page design you require.

1 Enter the number of columns you want. Specify a Gutter – the space between columns. InDesign calculates the widths of columns based on the overall width of the page, the number of columns, and the values entered for margins and gutters.

2 When working in a document, to change margin and column settings for the currently selected master page, spread or page, choose Layout>Margins and Columns. Enter new values as required. OK the dialog box.

The Working Environment

In common with Adobe Photoshop and Adobe Illustrator, Adobe InDesign is virtually identical on both the Windows and Macintosh platforms, making it easy to work in both environments without the need for extensive retraining.

This book uses a mixture of Windows and Macintosh screenshots, and the instructions given apply equally to both platforms. The identical functionality of InDesign on both platforms can be seen from an examination of the application windows on these pages, and from a comparison of the screenshots of various Windows and Macintosh dialog boxes and panels throughout the book.

Use the Zoom level pop-up menu to select a zoom level, or enter a value in the entry box then press Enter/ Return to change the zoom level

Drag the Zero Point crosshairs onto the page to reset the zero point

The Panel dock runs down the right edge of the InDesign window

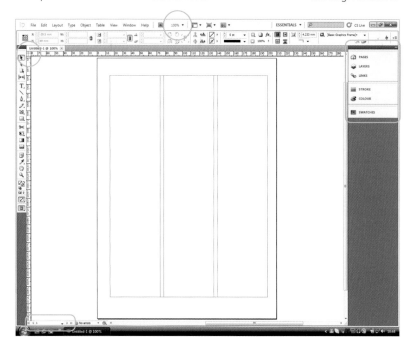

The Page Controls allow you to move to the Next/ Previous, First/Last pages in a multi-page document, or any page you specify in the Page Number field

InDesign CS4 and CS5 have a Workspace Switcher pop-up menu that includes preset arrangements of panels suitable for particular kinds of work

Click on a panel icon in the Panel dock to expand the panel, along with other panels in the same panel group

To avoid any confusion, it is good practice to delete unnecessary items from the pasteboard before you send your document to a commercial printer.

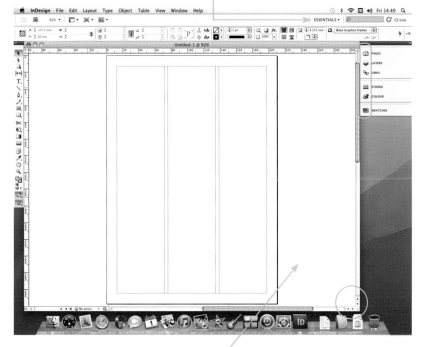

In InDesign CS5, click the CS Live button, provided you have an internet connection, to sign up for Adobe Online services which include file sharing, web conferencing and online review facilities.

13

The Pasteboard area exists all around the document page or spread. Objects you place on the Pasteboard are saved with the document but do not print

Click the Scroll Arrows to scroll the page up, down, left or right in increments. You can drag the Scroll Box to move the page a custom amount. Alternatively, click either side of the Scroll Box to move the window in half-screen increments

Application Bar: CS4, CS5

InDesign CS4 and CS5 have an Application bar with a button to launch Adobe Bridge and a convenient set of pop-up menus: Zoom Level, View Options, Screen Mode and Arrange Documents.

Each time you launch InDesign the Welcome screen appears. Click one of the listed links, or click the Close button to begin working in InDesign. To prevent the Welcome screen appearing every time you launch InDesign, deselect the Show this dialog at startup checkbox.

The Tool Panel CS5

Use the following techniques to choose tools and to work quickly and efficiently as you build page layouts in Adobe InDesign.

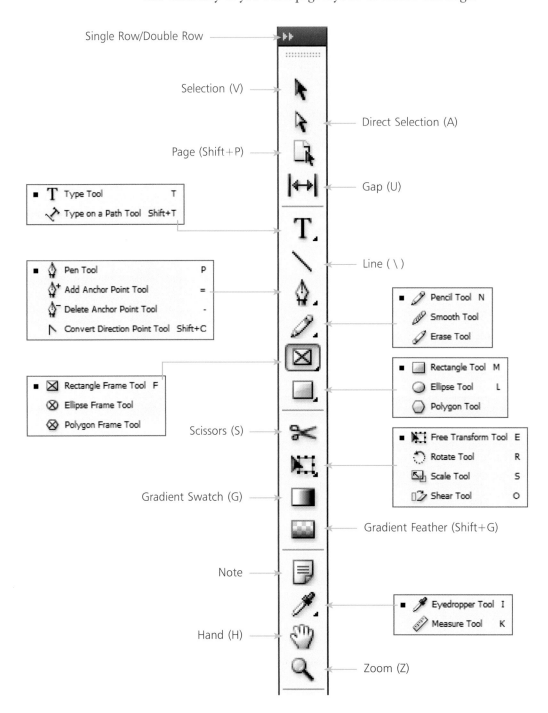

Single Row/Double Row

Selection (V)

Direct Selection (A)

Page (Shift+P)

Gap (U)

■ T Type Tool   T
↙ Type on a Path Tool   Shift+T

Line (\ )

■ ✎ Pen Tool   P
✎⁺ Add Anchor Point Tool   =
✎⁻ Delete Anchor Point Tool   -
⊾ Convert Direction Point Tool   Shift+C

■ ✐ Pencil Tool   N
✐ Smooth Tool
✐ Erase Tool

■ ⊠ Rectangle Frame Tool   F
⊗ Ellipse Frame Tool
⊗ Polygon Frame Tool

■ ▢ Rectangle Tool   M
◯ Ellipse Tool   L
⬡ Polygon Tool

Scissors (S)

■ ▦ Free Transform Tool   E
◌ Rotate Tool   R
▧ Scale Tool   S
▱ Shear Tool   O

Gradient Swatch (G)

Gradient Feather (Shift+G)

Note

■ ✐ Eyedropper Tool   I
📏 Measure Tool   K

Hand (H)

Zoom (Z)

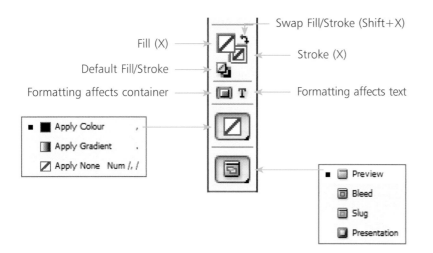

Fill (X)

Default Fill/Stroke

Formatting affects container

Swap Fill/Stroke (Shift+X)

Stroke (X)

Formatting affects text

- ■ Apply Colour ,
- Apply Gradient .
- Apply None Num /, /

- ■ Preview
- Bleed
- Slug
- Presentation

Tool Panel Techniques

1 Most of the time you will have the Tool panel visible as you build documents. If you accidentally close it, choose Window>Tools to display the Tool panel.

2 To choose a tool, click on it in the Tool panel. The tool is highlighted and when you move your cursor back into the InDesign window, the cursor changes to indicate the tool you selected.

3 A small, black triangle in the bottom-right corner of a tool icon indicates that there are additional tools available in the tool group. To access a hidden tool, press and hold the tool currently showing in the Tool panel; this will show the tool group pop-up. Slide your cursor onto the tool you want to select, and then release. The tool you select is displayed in the Tool panel as the default tool in that group until you choose another tool from the group.

4 Provided that you do not have the text insertion point located in text, press the Tab key to hide all visible panels including the Tool panel. Press Tab again to show all previously visible panels. Hold down Shift and press the Tab key to hide all panels except the Tool panel.

5 Rest your cursor on a tool in the Tool panel for a few seconds to display the tool tip label. This tells you the name of the tool and, in brackets, its keyboard shortcut.

Pen Tool (P)

15

Opening Documents

Hot tip

InDesign documents have the extension .indd. InDesign templates have the extension .indt.

As well as creating new InDesign documents, you will often need to open existing documents. If you open an InDesign document created by an earlier version of the software, InDesign converts the document to the version you are using and adds "[Converted]" to the document tab. When you save a converted file you are prompted to perform a Save As to save an updated copy of the file using the newer version of the software.

1 To open an existing document, choose File>Open.

2 Use standard Windows/Mac techniques to navigate to the file you want to open.

3 Click the file name to select it. Click the Open button.

4 In the Open a File dialog box, click the Copy radio button to open a copy of the file – the file opens as an untitled document.

5 When you want to edit an InDesign template, in the Open a File dialog box, click on the template file name and then select the Original radio button before you click Open.

Bridge

Adobe Bridge is a file management application providing a powerful, flexible set of controls which allow you to locate, track, view and manage all your digital assets created using Adobe Creative Suite applications as well as files created by other software applications. Click the Go to Bridge button in the Menu/ Application bar to launch Adobe Bridge.

Hot tip

You can launch Bridge as a standalone application – from the Start>Programs menu in Windows, or from the Applications folder on the Mac.

Favorites view

You can create your own favorites folders to provide quick access to folders you use on a regular basis.

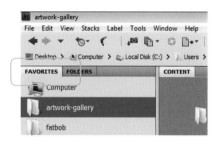

1   To create a new favorites folder, click the Favorites tab, then click the Computer icon. Navigate to the folder in the main Content pane by double-clicking folder icons. Position your cursor on the folder, then drag it into the Favorites pane, below the divider bar.

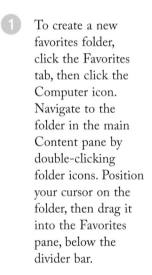

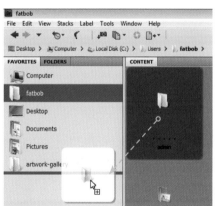

Hot tip

You can also create a Favorites folder from the Folders tab. Navigate to a folder, position your cursor on the folder then right-click (Windows) or ctrl+click (Mac). Select Add to Favorites from the context menu.

2   To remove a folder from the Favorites pane sidebar, position your cursor on the folder then right-click (Windows) or ctrl+click (Mac). Select Remove from Favorites from the context menu.

Folders View

In Folders view you can view, manage, sort and open files. You can also create new folders and move, rename, delete and rank files.

1   Click the Folders tab. Use the Folders pane to navigate to specific folders on your system using standard Windows/Macintosh techniques. You can also use the drop down list above the Folders tab to navigate to recently used folders.

...cont'd

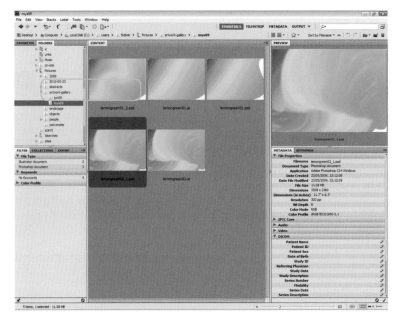

To move a file, position your cursor on the file thumbnail, then drag it to a different folder in the Folder panel of the Bridge window. To copy a file to a new location, hold down Ctrl (PC) or Alt/option (Mac), then drag it to a different folder.

 Thumbnail previews of the contents of the selected folder appear in the Contents pane in the middle of the window.

Essentials is the default Bridge workspace. Use the Workspace pop-up menu or click on one of the visible workspace options to change the arrangement of panes in Bridge to suit your needs.

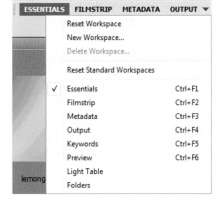

Click once on a file in the Content pane to display a larger preview in the Preview pane.
Position your cursor on any of the borders of the Preview pane, then drag to resize the pane as required.

To open a file from the content area, click on a thumbnail to select it, and then press Enter/Return. You can also double-click on a thumbnail.

Drag the Thumbnail Size slider at the bottom of the window, to increase or decrease the size of the thumbnail previews in the Contents pane.

6. To delete a file, click on the thumbnail to select it, and either click the Wastebasket icon in the Bridge Toolbar, or drag the thumbnail onto the Wastebasket. Alternatively, use Ctrl/Command+Delete.

7. To rank a thumbnail, first select it; then click one of the dots below the thumbnail image to award stars. You can add up to five stars. To remove stars, click one of the existing stars. Click to the left of the stars to remove all stars.

hk-china-images.indd

8. To display only thumbnails with a specific star rating, click the Filter tab to make it active, then click the Ratings expand triangle. Click to the left of a star rating to display files with that rating.

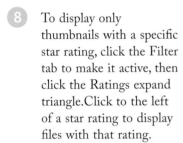

9. Click the Metadata or Keywords tab to view additional labeling information saved with a file. You can also use options from the panel menu ( ) for each tab to add and edit metadata and keyword information for the file. For selected InDesign files there are panes for Fonts and color swatches used in the document. Use the Expand/Collapse triangle (▶) to display/hide information for each category.

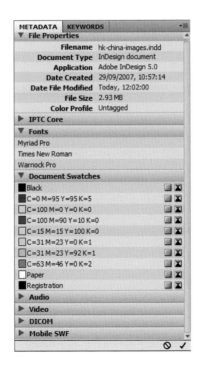

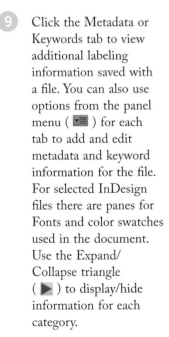
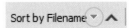

Mini Bridge

Mini Bridge provides a similar range of functionality to Adobe Bridge, but from within the InDesign working environment. Choose Window>Mini Bridge to show the panel.

① Click the Browse Files button to begin using Mini Bridge. Clicking the Browse Files button also launches Bridge in the background as Mini Bridge operations rely on Bridge to carry out tasks.

② Use the Panel View pop-up menu to control the visibility of the Path Bar and the Navigation and Preview Pods.

③ Use the Path Bar to navigate to folders containing files that you want to view in the panel. You can also use the Navigation Pod to move to folders on your system.

④ Drag the Thumbnail Size slider, at the bottom of the panel, to control the size of thumbnail previews in the Content Pod.

⑤ Click the View button at the bottom of the panel to specify the arrangement and appearance of file thumbnails.

6 To open an InDesign document from Mini Bridge double-click the thumbnail icon.

7 To place an image into the currently active InDesign document drag an image thumbnail onto the InDesign page. When you release the mouse button the Loaded Graphics cursor

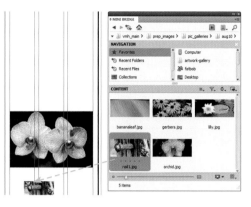

appears. You can now place the image (see page 88 for further information on placing images). When you place an image from Mini Bridge, InDesign forms a link to the image as it does when you use the File>Place command.

8 To see a larger preview for a selected image thumbnail in the Preview Pod, hold down Shift then press the Spacebar. Click the Close button to return to thumbnails view.

9 To see a full screen preview of a selected image, press the Spacebar. Press the Spacebar again to return to InDesign.

Beware

If you double-click an image thumbnail in Mini Bridge the image opens in Photoshop.

Hot tip

You can also use the Tools button ( ) in the Content bar to place the selected thumbnail. Click the Tools button, then select Place>In InDesign.

Hot tip

To see a full screen slideshow of all images in the Preview Pod, make sure that none of the images are selected. Click the Slideshow button ( ). Whilst the slideshow is running, press H on the keyboard to display on-screen commands for controlling the slideshow.

Workspaces and Panels

Workspaces

Your workspace is the arrangement of panels and document windows that you use as you create and work on InDesign documents. There is a wide variety of techniques for managing your workspace so that you work comfortably, efficiently and in a way that suits your own individual preferences. You can also save a workspace so that you can quickly and easily recreate a particular arrangement of panels.

InDesign CS3 does not have a Workspace pop-up menu available in the Application bar along the top edge of the InDesign window. All other functionality for managing and arranging panels and the workspace applies to this earlier version.

Hot tip

Choose Window> Workspace>New Workspace to save the current position of the panels. Enter a name for this workspace arrangement in the Save Workspace dialog box. To reset panels to this arrangement select the workspace name from the Workspace pop-up menu.
   In InDesign CS3 choose Window>Workspace to select a custom workspace.

1. Use the Workspace pop-up menu in the Applications bar to choose a default arrangement of panels to suit your requirements. You can modify a default workspace using techniques outlined below to create a custom workspace.

2. To revert a modified workspace to the default arrangement you can select Reset <name of workspace> from the workspace pop-up menu.

Managing panels

Much of InDesign's functionality is accessed through panels: you can work with floating panels or with panels in the vertical Panel dock that runs down the right edge of the InDesign window. Floating or docked panels always appear in front of the document pages. The majority of the panels are organized initially into combined groups, but you can create your own groupings if necessary. The following techniques will help you customize the way you work with panels and the Panel docks.

Don't forget

All panels can be found in the Window menu. The Type menu also allows you to display panels for Character, Paragraph, Character Styles, Paragraph Styles, Tabs and Story. When you choose a panel, it displays along with any other panels currently in its group.

1. Click the Expand panels button (◀◀) to display expanded panel groups. Click the Collapse to Icons button (▶▶) to shrink the dock to icons and labels. Position your cursor on the left edge of the Panel dock, when the cursor changes to the bidirectional arrow (⟷), drag to the right to create an icons only dock. Drag to the left to expand the dock manually.

2. For a collapsed dock, click on a panel in the Panel dock to display the panel and panels in the same group. The panel remains anchored to the Panel dock. Click on the same panel tab to collapse the panel group back into the dock.

③ For an expanded dock, to make a panel active, click its tab. The tab highlights and the options for the panel are displayed.

④ To move a floating panel, such as Align, position your cursor in the title bar of the panel; then press and drag. To close a floating panel, click once on the Close button in the title bar of the panel.

⑤ Double-click the panel tab name to cycle through panel views: with options, without options, tab only. You can also double-click a panel's title bar to completely collapse it, or to restore it to its previous state.

Panel groups

Some panels appear as groups when you select them from the Window menu. For example, Align and Pathfinder appear initially as a floating panel group. Use the following techniques to control the appearance of panel groups.

① To hide all panels in a group, click the group's Close button (▨). Select any of the panels from the Window menu to redisplay the complete panel group.

② Click the Collapse to Icons button to reduce the display of the panel group to and icons and labels. Click the Expand Panels button to return to the previous display state of the panel.

Floating and combining panels

You can convert panels in the dock into floating panels and vice versa.

① Drag the panel tab name out of a panel group to create a stand-alone, floating panel.

② Drag a panel name tab into another panel group or individual panel to create a new custom panel group. When combining panels, release the mouse button when the panel you are dragging into highlights with a blue border. You can also drag the tab of a floating panel into one of the Panel dock groups to combine it with the group.

The Control Panel

Don't forget

The Control panel menu button ( ) is located to the far right of the panel.

The Control panel is one of the most versatile panels in InDesign. The default position for the panel is docked below the Menu bar. It provides convenient access to an extensive range of settings and controls, which change depending on the tool you are working with and the object you have selected.

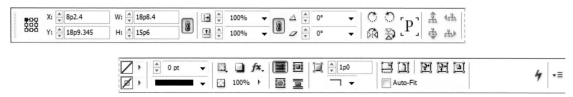

CS5: Graphic/Shape frame selected with Selection tool

CS5: Text frame selected with Type tool

Beware

As with other panels and dialog boxes in InDesign, if you make a change to a setting with nothing selected, that setting becomes the default for objects you subsequently create. For example, if you use options in the Control panel to change the font to Arial and the type size to 72pt, the next time you create a text frame, text you enter appears with these settings. This is a useful and powerful feature, but in the early stages of learning the application be careful that it doesn't catch you out.

① When you are working in a text frame with the Type tool selected, you can choose between the Character Formatting Controls button and the Paragraph Formatting Controls button as required.

Control Panel: CS3, CS4

The set of options available in the Control panel has changed slightly in CS5 compared to earlier versions.

For example, the Go to Bridge button found in the CS3 Control Panel is now found in the Application bar in CS5; whilst new Fill and Stroke options are now present in the CS5 Control panel, which were not available in previous versions.

However, the broad principles of using the Control Panel remain consistent: depending on what you have selected the panel provides access to a wide range of the most useful controls for working with and manipulating the selected object.

Ruler Guides

Ruler guides are non-printing guides that are used to align objects accurately. The default color for ruler guides is light blue. When Snap to Guides is on, drawing tool cursors snap onto guides when they come within four screen pixels of the guide. Also, when you move an object, the edges of the object will snap onto guides.

① To create a ruler guide, make sure the rulers are showing; choose View>Show Rulers (Ctrl/Command+R) if they are not. Position your cursor in either the top or the left ruler; then press and drag onto the page. When you release, you create a ruler guide at that point. Look at the Control panel or the Transform panel X/Y fields to get a readout indicating the position of the cursor as you press and drag.

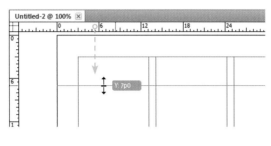

② To create a ruler guide that runs across both pages in a spread, double-click in the ruler at the point at which you want the guide. Alternatively, drag from a ruler but release the mouse when the cursor is on the pasteboard area surrounding the page.

③ To reposition a ruler guide, select the Selection tool, position your cursor on an existing guide; then press and drag. A double-headed arrow cursor appears, indicating that you have picked up the guide.

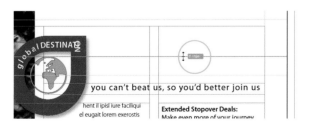

④ To remove a ruler guide, select the Selection tool and then click on the guide. It changes color, indicating that it is selected. Press the Backspace or Delete key. Alternatively, drag the guide back into the ruler it came from.

Hot tip

You can switch Snap to Guides off by choosing View>Grids & Guides>Snap to Guides. A tick mark next to the command indicates that Snap to Guides is on:

✓ Snap to Guides   Shift+Ctrl+;

Hot tip

A "spread" usually consists of two pages – a left- and a right-hand page – viewed side by side. For example, when you read a magazine or a book, you are viewing spreads.

Hot tip

Click the right mouse button (Windows), or ctrl+click (Mac) on the vertical or horizontal ruler to change the ruler units via a context-sensitive menu.

...cont'd

Beware

In a document with multiple layers, ruler guides appear on the active layer. When you hide the layer you also hide the layer's ruler guides. (See page 103, "Understanding Layers".)

Hot tip

Provided that the Show Transformation Values checkbox is selected (Edit/InDesign> Preferences>Interface) an on-screen measurements label readout appears at the cursor as you create or move a ruler guide.

Hot tip

Use the keyboard shortcut Ctrl/Com+Alt+G to select all guides on a page or spread.

Hot tip

To lock guides on a specific layer, select the layer then choose Layer Options for … from the Layers panel menu, or double click the layer in Layers panel. Select the Lock Guides option.

5 To position a guide with complete precision, drag in a guide and position it roughly where you want it. Click on the guide with the Selection tool; then enter the position you want in the X or Y entry field in the Control panel or the Transform panel. Press Enter/Return to apply the new value.

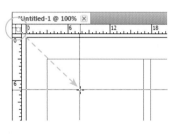

6 To create a vertical and horizontal guide simultaneously, position your cursor in the crosshair area, where the vertical and horizontal rulers meet. Hold down Ctrl/Command, then

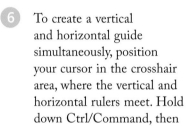

press and drag onto the page. Release the mouse button before you release the Ctrl/Command key, otherwise you will reposition the Zero point.

Hiding/Showing and Locking/Unlocking Guides

1 To lock an individual guide, click on it with the Selection tool to select it. The guide changes color to indicate that it is selected. Then choose Object>Lock (Ctrl/Command+L). If you try to move the guide, a padlock icon appears indicating the guide's locked status. To unlock a locked guide, click on it to select it; then choose Object>Unlock All on Spread (Ctrl/Command+Alt/option+L). This option also unlocks any locked objects on the page or spread at the same time.

2 To lock all the guides for the entire document, regardless of what layer they are on, choose View>Grid & Guides>Lock Guides (Ctrl/Command+Alt/option+ ;). A tick mark next to the option in the menu indicates that guides are locked. Use the same option to unlock guides.

3 To hide/show all ruler guides as well as margin and column guides, choose View>Grids & Guides>Hide/Show Guides (Ctrl/ Command+ ;). This command does not hide frame edge guides, which define the size and position of frames on a page. Choose View>Extras>Hide/Show Frame Edges (Ctrl+H – Windows, Command+Alt/option+H – Mac) to hide/show frame edges.

Saving Documents

It is important to be able to use the Save As, Save and Save a Copy commands as necessary. To avoid losing work, save soon after you start working on a document and remember to save regularly as you make changes.

Save As

Use the Save As command soon after starting a new document. Save As enables you to specify a folder and name for the document.

1 To save a file for the first time, choose File>Save As (Ctrl/Command+Shift+S). Use standard Windows/Mac dialog boxes to specify the folder into which you want to save the document.

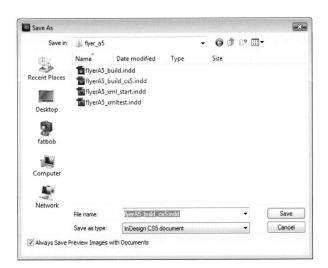

2 Make sure the File name entry field is highlighted. Enter a name for the document. Leave the Save As Type pop-up (Windows), or Format pop-up (Mac), set to InDesign CS5 Document. Click on Save. The name of the document appears in the document name tab or the title bar of the InDesign document window.

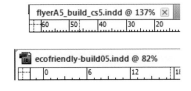

Save

Use the Save command regularly as you build your InDesign document, so that changes you make are not accidentally lost due to any system or power failure. Each time you use the Save command,

Hot tip

You can also use the Save As command when you want to create a new version of the document on which you are working. Use File>Save As, specify a different location and/or enter a different name for the file. When you OK the Save As dialog box you continue to work on the new file; the original remains as it was when you last saved it.

Hot tip

Use the shortcut Ctrl/Command+Alt/option+Shift+S to save all open documents at the same time.

Hot tip

To revert to the last saved version of a file, choose File>Revert. Confirm the revert in the warning dialog box. The file reverts to the stage it was at when you last used the Save command. This option can sometimes be more efficient than using repeated Undo commands.

...cont'd

Hot tip

Choose File>Close when you finish working on a document. If you have not already saved the file, in the warning box that appears, click Save to save and close the file, click Cancel to return to the document without saving, or click Don't Save to close the document without saving any changes.

Beware

When saving InDesign files avoid using reserved characters such as: / \ : ; * ? < > , $ %. Reserved characters can have special meanings in some operating systems and can cause problems when files are used on different platforms.

changes you have made to the document are added to the already saved version of the file. You do not need to rename the file or specify its location every time you use the Save command.

1. To save a file, choose File>Save (Ctrl/Command+S) at regular intervals as you build your document.

Save A Copy

Use the Save a Copy command to save a copy of the document at its present state. When you have saved a copy, you continue to work on the original file, not the copy.

1. To save a copy of a document at its present state, choose File>Save a Copy. Use standard Windows/Mac dialog boxes to specify the folder into which you want to save the document. Make sure the File name entry field is highlighted. Enter a name for the document. Click the Save button. The copy is saved in the location and with the name specified. You continue to work on the original file.

Saving Templates

Save a document as a template when you want to create a series of documents with consistent layout, text formatting, color and graphic elements. For example, if you are creating a monthly newsletter, set up an InDesign document that contains all of the standard guides, master pages, style sheets, colors, placeholder frames and graphics. Each time you begin a new issue, open the template and import new content into the existing structure; this will ensure consistency from month to month.

1. To save a document as a template, follow the steps for the Save As command, but choose InDesign ... template from the Save as type pop-up (Windows), the Format pop-up (Mac).

Zooming and Scrolling

Use the Zoom tool, the Zoom level pop-up menu and a variety of keyboard shortcuts for changing the zoom level as you work on a document. You can use the Hand tool and the scroll bars for moving around the document.

1. To use the Zoom tool, select it, position the zoom cursor in the document window, and then click to zoom in at the cursor position by preset increments. With the Zoom tool selected, hold down Alt/option to change the cursor to the zoom out cursor. Click to zoom out by preset decrements.

2. One powerful zoom technique is to press and drag with the Zoom tool to define an area on which you want to zoom. A dotted rectangle appears, defining the zoom area. The smaller the zoom area you define, the greater the resulting magnification.

3. You can use standard scroll bar techniques to see different parts of a page, or you can use the Hand tool: select the Hand tool, position your cursor on the page, and then press and drag to scroll the page.

4. You can zoom to preset percentage levels using the Zoom Level pop-up in the Application bar along the top edge of the InDesign workspace.

100% ▼
5%
12.5%
25%
50%
75%
✓ 100%
125%
150%
200%
300%

5. The View menu offers standard options for changing the magnification of the page. The keyboard shortcut is listed with each option.

Zoom In	Ctrl+=
Zoom Out	Ctrl+-
✓ Fit Page in Window	Ctrl+0
Fit Spread in Window	Alt+Ctrl+0
Actual Size	Ctrl+1
Entire Pasteboard	Alt+Shift+Ctrl+0

Hot tip

With any tool other than the Zoom tool selected, hold down Ctrl/Command+Spacebar to temporarily access the Zoom tool. Add Alt/option to the above combination to access the zoom out option.

Hot tip

With any tool other than the Hand tool selected, hold down the Spacebar on the keyboard to gain temporary access to the Hand tool. If you are working with the Type tool, hold down Alt/option to access the Hand tool, otherwise you will introduce spaces at the text insertion point.

In InDesign CS3 the Zoom Level pop-up menu is in the bottom left corner of the InDesign workspace.

Navigator Panel: CS3

InDesign CS3 includes a Navigator panel (Window>Object & Layout>Navigator) for zooming in and out and for scrolling around in a document.

Enter a value in the Zoom % entry field; then press Return/Enter to apply it. Or, drag the zoom slider to the right or left to zoom in and out.

Drag the red View box to move quickly to other parts of the page.

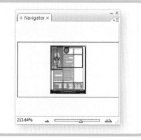

Page Tool

> The Page tool is a new feature introduced in InDesign CS5.

The Page tool is useful if you want to create multiple pages of different sizes within the same InDesign document. This can be convenient if you want to create and manage corporate identity documents such as a business card, letterhead and compliments slip which share the same logo, address and contact details and other branding elements within a single document rather than trying to manage and update several separate files to maintain consistency.

You can also use multiple page sizes to create gatefold layouts for magazines and brochures.

 To create a custom page size, select the Page tool. Click on a page in the document window, not the Pages panel, to select it. A light blue highlight indicates that the page is selected.

Hot tip

Choose Layout>Margins and Columns to set appropriate margin and column settings for the new custom page size if necessary.

Use the Width (W) and Height (H) fields in the Control panel to specify dimensions for the page. Or, choose a preset page size from the Page Size pop-up menu in the Control panel.

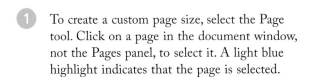

If you are working with a spread, creating a gatefold, you can use the X and Y fields to control the position of the custom page relative to other pages in the spread.

Hot tip

By basing pages of different sizes on the same master you only have to edit an element, such as contact details, once on the master for all page types based on that master to update.

Switch on Show Master Page overlay to display a blue frame representing the dimensions of the master page, so that you can reposition master page objects to a suitable position on a custom page. Then, position your Page tool cursor on the highlighted edge of the overlay and drag. For example, for a logo placed in the top left corner of a letterhead you need to drag the master page overlay to display the logo within the smaller page size of a business card.

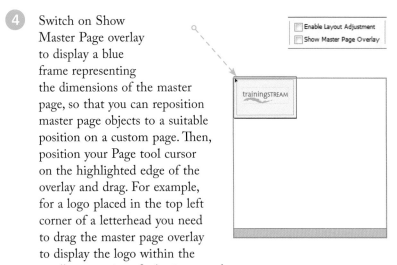

2 Building Pages

This chapter shows you how to create, manipulate and control text and graphic frames, lines and basic shapes to achieve the exact page layout structure you require.

Creating Frames

Don't forget

The Type tool draws from the baseline indicator (the bar that crosses the I-beam about three quarters of the way down the cursor) not from the top of the cursor:

Hot tip

See page 46 for information on working with the Live Corners box (□) that appears when you select a rectangle shape or text frame with the Selection tool. Ellipses, polygons and stars do not have corner controls.

The Frame tools create containers, which define areas on your page that will hold text or images. You can construct the basic layout of a page using frames before you import text and images, or you create a frame and begin to work with its content immediately.

There are three sets of tools you can use to create frames. The Rectangle Frame, Ellipse Frame and Polygon Frame tools create frames into which you can place images. The Rectangle, Ellipse and Polygon tools allow you to create shape frames. Typically, you use shape frames to create simple graphic objects on your page. You can use the Type tool to create text frames into which you can type or import text.

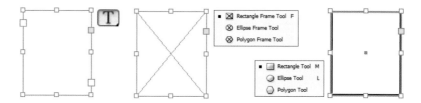

Empty text frames display in- and out-ports at the upper left and lower right corners, respectively, when selected with the Selection tool. Empty graphic frames display an X running through the middle (provided that View>Extras>Show Frame Edges is selected). Empty shape frames initially have a default 1 point black stroke and no fill.

1   To draw a frame, select the appropriate tool; the cursor changes to the drawing tool cursor. Press and drag away from the start point, and release when the frame is the size you want. Don't worry if you don't get the shape exactly right to begin with – you can always resize and reposition the frame at a later stage.

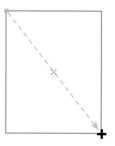

2   When you release the mouse button, the shape is "selected" – it appears in a "bounding box" which has eight selection handles around the outside. The selection bounding box disappears when you deselect the object. A basic shape frame takes on any fill and/or stroke attributes currently set in the

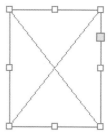

Tool panel. (See page 116 for information on working with fill and stroke.) Unlike basic shapes, a graphic frame does not take on any fill and/or stroke attributes currently set in the Tool panel. By default, graphic frames are ready to hold an imported image or graphic.

3 To draw a square or circular frame hold down the Shift key, and then press and drag away from the start point. The Shift key acts as a constraint on the drawing tool. Make sure you release the mouse button before the Shift key, otherwise the constraint is lost. You can also use the Shift key with the Polygon tool to maintain its proportions.

4 To draw a frame from the center out, hold down the Alt/option key before you start to drag to create the frame.

5 After you draw an object, you can continue to draw further objects, because the drawing tool remains selected. Make sure you choose the Selection tool if you want to make changes to the size or position of an object.

6 To delete a frame, select it with the Selection tool and then press the Backspace or Delete key on your keyboard.

Polygon tools

Use the Polygon Frame tool and the Polygon tool to draw regular polygons or stars. Use the Polygon Settings dialog box to specify the Number of Sides for a polygon, or the number of points for a star. Use the Star Inset to create a star and control the width of the spokes on the star. A Star Inset value of zero creates a polygon.

1 To specify the number of sides in a Polygon or a Star Inset to create a Star, double-click one of the Polygon tools. Enter values as required. OK the dialog box, and then press and drag to create the shape using these settings.

Polygon Settings

Options

Number of Sides: 5

Star Inset: 50%

OK

Cancel

33

Selection Techniques

A fundamental technique in any page layout application is that of selecting objects before you make changes to them. In Adobe InDesign, you use the Selection tool to select and deselect objects.

An object in InDesign is any shape created with one of the basic shape drawing tools, any frame created with one of the frame tools, a line created with the Line tool, or any path created with the Pen or Pencil tool. Objects are the fundamental building blocks of all InDesign documents.

 Make sure you have the Selection tool selected. Click on an object to select it. With the exception of horizontal or vertical lines, a blue bounding box with eight selection handles appears around the object, indicating that it is selected.

A selection bounding box represents the horizontal and vertical dimensions of an object. The eight selection handles allow you to change the width and/or height of the object. Rectangular graphic and text frames also display a yellow box that allows you to access Live Corner controls (see page 46 for further information). Vertical/ Horizontal lines have selection handles at both ends.

Beware

34

If a shape frame does not have a fill you can only select it by clicking on its path (the edge) – it is not selected if you click inside the shape.

2 To deselect one or more objects, click into some empty space with the Selection tool, or choose Edit>Deselect All (Ctrl/Command+Shift+A).

| Select All | Ctrl+A |
| Deselect All | Shift+Ctrl+A |

Don't forget

The Selection tool is used to select, resize and move objects or groups. The Direct Selection tool is used to edit the shape of paths or frames by working directly on the anchor points that form the shape. The Direct Selection tool is also used for working on the contents of graphic frames.

3 To select more than one object, click on the first object to select it, hold down the Shift key, and then click on additional objects to add

them to the selection. Multiple objects selected in this manner form a temporary grouping: if you move one of the objects, the other selected objects move, maintaining the relative position of each object. This temporary grouping is lost as soon as you select a different object, or click in some empty space.

4. Another technique for selecting multiple objects is to marquee select them. With the Selection tool selected, position your cursor so that it is not touching any object on the page. Press and drag; as you do so a dotted marquee box appears. Any object that this marquee touches will be selected when you release the mouse button. This is a very powerful selection technique, and it is worth practising it a few times to become familiar with it.

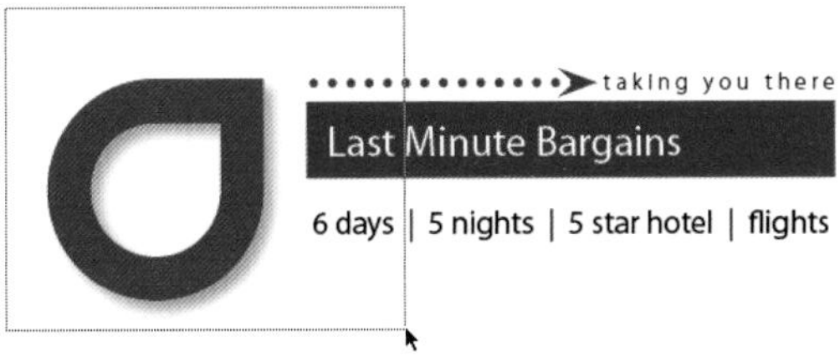
taking you there
Last Minute Bargains
6 days | 5 nights | 5 star hotel | flights

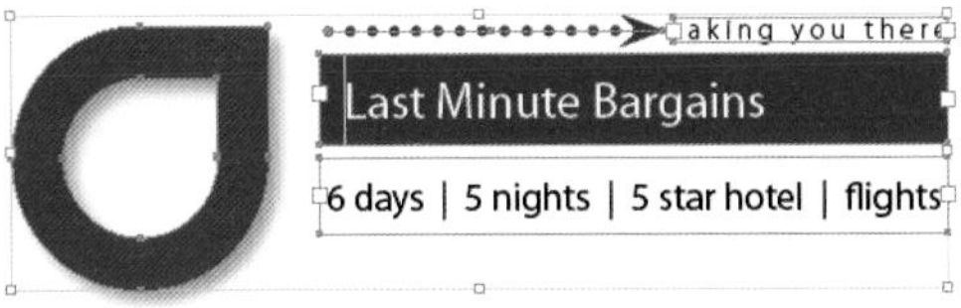
taking you there
Last Minute Bargains
6 days | 5 nights | 5 star hotel | flights

5. With any tool selected you can choose Edit>Select All (Ctrl/Command+A) to select all objects on the currently active page or spread, as well as on the pasteboard area surrounding the page.

Late Season Specials
6 days / 5 nights / 5 star hotel / flights
ISTANBUL
globalTRAVELNATION:
travel with a light footstep

6. The Select sub-menu provides useful controls for selecting objects in complex areas of overlapping objects. Select an object, and choose Edit>Select to access the options in the sub-menu. (See page 100 for further information on changing the stacking order of objects.)

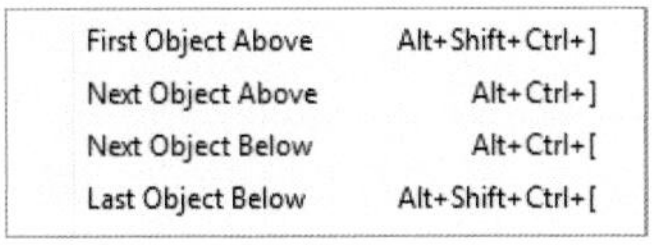
First Object Above Alt+Shift+Ctrl+]
Next Object Above Alt+Ctrl+]
Next Object Below Alt+Ctrl+[
Last Object Below Alt+Shift+Ctrl+[

Hot tip

Select an empty text, graphic or shape frame; then choose Object>Content to access the frame type sub-menu. Choose from Graphic, Text or Unassigned to convert the frame to a different type:

Graphic
Text
Unassigned

Beware

The Select All command does not select objects on locked or hidden layers.

Moving Objects

You can move objects anywhere you want on the pages of your document or onto the pasteboard area surrounding your pages. Objects can cross over margins, and you can create a "bleed" by positioning an object so that it runs across the edge of a page onto the pasteboard.

1 To move or reposition an object, select the Selection tool, position your cursor inside the object, and then press and drag to move the object to a new location. If you are moving an image, make sure you don't position your cursor on the Content Grabber which appears at the centre of the image. (See below for further information.)

2 To constrain the movement to vertical, horizontal or increments of 45 degrees, hold down Shift and then press and drag to reposition the object. Remember to release the mouse button before you release the Shift key, otherwise the constraining effect of the Shift key is lost.

3 To move an object in increments, make sure that the object is selected, and then press the up, down, left and right arrow keys on the keyboard. Each time you press an arrow key the object moves .25mm. To change the nudge increment, choose Edit>Preferences>Units & Increments (Windows), or InDesign>Preferences>Units & Increments (Mac). Enter a new value in the Cursor Key entry field. Hold down Shift while pressing an arrow key to move an object 10 times the Cursor Key setting.

Content Grabber: CS5

When moving images with the Selection tool in CS5, be careful that you don't drag the "Content Grabber".

The Content Grabber appears at the centre of the image when you move the Selection tool over an image. You can use the Grabber to reposition the image within the frame without first having to select the Direct Selection tool. (See page 91 for further information.) The Content Grabber moves the image inside a frame, not the frame itself.

Manually Resizing Objects

Once you've drawn an object you can resize it manually using the Selection tool. You can resize basic objects, open paths, graphic and text frames and groups.

① To resize a basic shape or frame, select the Selection tool. Click on the object; the object is highlighted and eight selection handles appear around the outside. An irregularly shaped object appears within a blue rectangular bounding box with handles.

② Drag the centre left/right handle to increase/decrease only the width of the object. Drag the center top/bottom handle to resize only the height. Drag a corner handle to resize width and height simultaneously.

③ To maintain the proportions of an object or group as you resize it, hold down Shift and drag a selection handle.

④ To resize a line drawn at an angle, select it using the Selection tool. Notice that dragging a handle changes the start or end position of the line, in effect changing the length of the line. To change the thickness of a line use the Stroke panel. (See pages 39–40 for further information on using the Stroke panel.)

⑤ When you manually resize an object using the Selection tool, the Stroke weight remains constant.

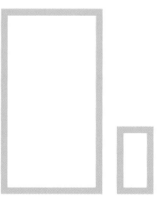

CS3 & CS4

For basic shapes and paths, if you press and drag on a selection handle in one movement, you see a blue bounding box that represents the new size of the object:

If you press on the selection handle, pause momentarily, and then drag, you see a representation of the complete shape as you resize it:

When you use this technique on an object with Text Wrap applied to it, you see a live preview of text reflowing as you change the size of the object.

When you resize an object in CS4 and CS5, an on-screen readout of Width and Height dimensions appears at the cursor as you drag, making it easy to resize objects to precise dimensions:

W: 9p0
H: 9p0

Control and Transform Panels

When you need to manipulate an object with numerical accuracy you can use the Control panel or the Transform panel. When you select an object with the Selection tool, these panels display a range of controls for manipulating it.

The matrix of small squares to the left of the panels are the reference points. Each point refers to a corresponding handle on the bounding box of the object. There is also a reference point for the center of the object. Click on a reference point to specify the point around which the transformation takes place.

1 The X and Y entry fields allow you to position an object precisely. The X value specifies the position of the object's reference point from the left edge of the page or spread. The Y value specifies the position of the object's reference point from the top of the page.

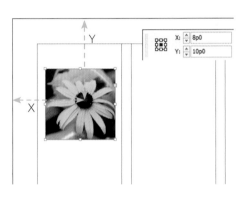

2 To scale an empty text, graphic or shape object to exact dimensions, enter precise values in the W/H entry fields. Provided that the Constrain Proportions icon is selected, when you change either the Width or Height value, the other value updates automatically to scale the object in proportion.

3 To scale a frame and its contents (picture or text) as a percentage, enter a scale value in the percentage entry fields, or use the pop-up to choose a preset value. To scale the width, use the Scale X Percentage field; to scale the height use the Scale Y Percentage field. You can also enter precise amounts in the Scale

X/Y Percentage fields (e.g. 12p6). Provided that the Constrain Proportions icon is selected, when you change either the Width or Height value, the other value updates automatically to scale the object in proportion.

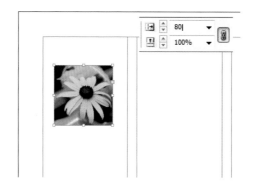

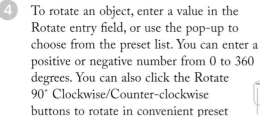

4. To rotate an object, enter a value in the Rotate entry field, or use the pop-up to choose from the preset list. You can enter a positive or negative number from 0 to 360 degrees. You can also click the Rotate 90° Clockwise/Counter-clockwise buttons to rotate in convenient preset amounts.

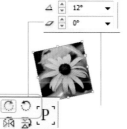

Hot tip

You can also use the Rotate tool to rotate selected objects or frames manually.

5. To shear an object, enter a value in the Shear entry field, or use the pop-up to choose from the preset list.

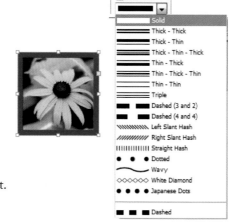

6. To apply a stroke to an object, click into the Stroke Weight field and then enter a value, or choose a value from the Stroke Weight list. Choose a style for the stroke from the Stroke Type pop-up list.

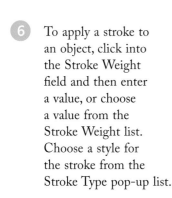

Hot tip

...cont'd

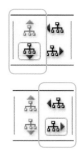

7. When you select a graphic frame that contains an image, click the Select Container or Select Content button to toggle the selection status between the frame and the image inside.

8. Select an object using the Selection tool, then use the Select Next/Previous Object buttons to cycle through and select objects on the page or spread. Hold down Shift then click a button to skip by 5 through objects on a page or spread.

9. You can use the Horizontal and Vertical Flip buttons to quickly flip objects. Get into the habit of checking which reference point is selected in the Control panel before you flip an object so that you don't end up with unexpected results. The examples below use the center reference point. The flip indicator to the right of the Flip buttons provides an excellent visual check for any flip setting applied to an object.

Fill and Stroke pop-up panels: CS5

You can quickly access the Swatches panel as a pop-up panel from the Control panel. Click either the Fill or Stroke triangle to apply color as required. (See pages 116–117 for further information on working with Fill and Stroke.)

Lines

Use the Line tool to create horizontal and vertical lines, or lines at any angle. You can modify lines using the Selection tools or using the Control or Transform panels. Use the Stroke panel to change line weight, to add arrow heads, and to create dashed or dotted lines.

1 To draw a horizontal or vertical line, select the Line tool. Position your cursor on the page, hold down the Shift key, and then press and drag. Release the mouse button before the Shift key when the line is the desired length. The line remains selected when you release, indicated by the two selection handles.

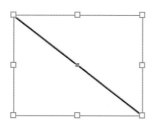

2 To edit a horizontal or vertical line, select the Selection tool, click on the line to select it, and drag one of the end points. The vertical/horizontal constraint remains in effect as you resize the line.

3 To draw a line at any angle across your page, select the Line tool, position your cursor on the page, and then press and drag. When you release, the line remains selected, indicated by a selection bounding box with eight selection handles.

4 To edit a line at any angle, select the Selection tool and then click the line to select it. The bounding box appears around the line. Drag any of the selection handles to change the start or end point of the line. Alternatively, select the line with the Direct Selection tool. Drag an end point to resize the line.

5 To change the thickness of a selected line, choose Window>Stroke (or click the Stroke icon in the Panel dock) to show the Stroke panel if it is not already showing. To change the thickness of the line, you can click the Weight increment buttons to change the thickness in single point increments, enter an exact value in the Weight entry box and press Enter/ Return, or choose a setting from the Weight pop-up list.

Hot tip

For any drawing tool, provided that View>Grids & Guides>Snap to Guides is selected, the drawing tool cursor snaps or locks onto a guide when it comes within four screen pixels of a column, margin or ruler guide. For graphic and shape frame tools, the cursor displays a hollow arrow head to indicate when it is snapping to a guide. Snap to Guides is useful when you need to create and position objects with precision.

Hot tip

To convert a horizontal or vertical line to an angled line, select it with the Direct Selection tool and then drag one of the end anchor points:

...cont'd

Lines and the Control panel

You can use the Control panel to control line attributes with numeric precision.

Hot tip

You can drag using the Pencil tool to draw freeform lines. The Smooth tool, in the Pencil tool group, allows you to make a path smoother by dragging across it. The Erase tool allows you to erase portions of a selected path by dragging across it.

1. Use the Selection tool to select the line you want to change. Click on the start, end or midpoint reference point for the line, to specify the point on the line to which changes refer.

2. Enter values in the X and Y entry fields to specify the exact position for the chosen reference point of the line.

3. Enter a value in the L entry field to specify the length of the line. Alternatively, use the Scale X Percentage and the Scale Y Percentage to change the length and thickness of the line; Scale X and Scale Y have the same effect on a line, provided that the Constrain Proportions for scaling button is selected.

Hot tip

See page 38 for information on working with coordinates.

4. Use the Rotate and Shear entry fields to rotate and shear the line. Shearing on a line becomes apparent when you increase its Stroke weight. (See pages 206 and 209 for further information on rotating and shearing objects.)

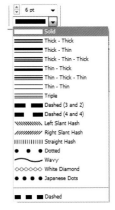

5. To apply a stroke to an object, click into the Stroke Weight field and then enter a value, or choose a value from the Stroke Weight list. Choose a style for the stroke from the Stroke Type pop-up list.

Hot tip

You can use the Transform panel to change line attributes with numeric precision. Choose Window>Object & Layout>Transform to show the panel. The controls available in the panel offer a convenient subset of those in the Control panel.

Stroke pop-up panel: CS5

To change the stroke color for a selected object using the Control panel, click the Stroke pop-up triangle to apply color as required. (See page 118 for further information on working with the Swatches panel.)

Cut, Copy, Paste, Clear

The Clipboard provides one of the most convenient and flexible methods for copying, cutting and pasting objects, frames, groups and text. The limitation of the clipboard is that it holds the result of only one cut or copy command at a time. As soon as you perform another cut or copy, the newly cut or copied object replaces the previous contents of the clipboard.

1. Use the Selection tool to select an object, frame or group; then choose Edit>Cut/Copy. Copy leaves the original on the page and places a copy of the selected object onto the clipboard. Cut removes the selected object from the page and places it on the clipboard.

Cut	Ctrl+X
Copy	Ctrl+C
Paste	Ctrl+V
Paste without Formatting	Shift+Ctrl+V
Paste Into	Alt+Ctrl+V
Paste in Place	Alt+Shift+Ctrl+V
Clear	Backspace

2. Highlight a range of text using the Type tool and then choose Edit>Cut/Copy to place selected text onto the clipboard. (See page 53, Chapter 3, for further information on copying and pasting text.)

3. To paste objects and frames that have been copied to the clipboard back into a document, make sure the Selection tool is selected, and choose Edit>Paste (Ctrl/Command+V). The contents of the clipboard are pasted into the center of your screen display.

4. Choose Edit>Clear (Backspace) for a selected object, frame or group to delete the selected object(s) from the document completely. The clear command does not use the clipboard and therefore does not affect its contents.

5. Choose Edit>Paste in Place (Ctrl/Command+Alt/ option+Shift+V) to paste an object or group onto a page in exactly the same position as that from which it was cut.

See page 53, Chapter 3

Don't forget

The Clipboard is a temporary, invisible storage area. If you cut an important object to the clipboard, paste it back into the document as soon as possible to minimize the risk of accidentally overwriting it with another cut or copy command.

Beware

The contents of the clipboard are not saved when you exit InDesign.

Hot tip

After you cut or copy an object or text to the clipboard, you can paste it any number of times into your document or into any other publication.

43

Smart Guides

Smart Guides appear automatically when you draw, resize, move and align objects on your page as you perform actions to build a layout. The benefit of working with Smart Guides is that you can work accurately from the start with less fine tuning to be done at a later stage. Smart Guides can also reduce the need to access dialog boxes and panels to achieve accurate and consistent positioning of objects.

1. To Hide/Show Smart Guides, choose View>Grid & Guides>Smart Guides (Ctrl/Com+U).

2. To control which types of Smart Guides appear when Smart Guides are switched on, choose Edit (Windows)/InDesign (Mac)>Preferences>Guides & Pasteboard. In the Smart Guide Options area, deselect Smart Guide checkboxes for any categories you don't want to appear.

Smart Guide Options	
☑ Align to Object Centre	☑ Smart Dimensions
☑ Align to Object Edges	☑ Smart Spacing

Drawing Objects using Smart Cursors/Smart Guides

When you draw objects using tools such as the Rectangle Frame tool, the Rectangle tool, the Line tool, the Pen tool and the Type tool, you can use Smart Cursors to draw new objects aligned to existing objects on the page. Also, Smart Guides display to indicate matching dimensions for objects.

1. To draw an object aligned to another object, select one of the object drawing tools. As you position your cursor to draw the new object watch the drawing cursor carefully. The appearance of a white triangle at the cursor indicates that the cursor aligns with an edge or the center of an existing object. Drag with the drawing tool. The start of the new object aligns accurately with the edge of the existing object:

Cursor not aligned

Cursor aligned with top edge of frame

New frame aligns with top edge of existing frame

2. To draw a frame to match the size of an existing frame, working with a frame tool, or the Type tool, position your cursor so that it is aligned with an edge of the existing frame. (See previous

technique.) Start to drag to define the size of the new frame. Vertical and Horizontal Smart Dimension guides appear to indicate that heights/widths match when the cursor reaches the correct position.

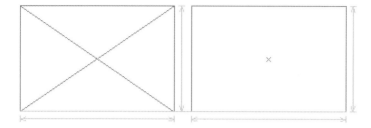

Positioning objects using Smart Guides

Smart Guides make it quick and easy to position and align an object to the center or edge of another other object, or the page. You can also create equal spacing between objects using Smart Spacing.

1 Make sure that Smart Guides are switched on. Using the Selection tool, start to drag an object across your page. Various Smart Spacing and Align guides appear as you reposition the object to indicate where objects align. In this screenshot, arrows on the right indicate equal vertical spacing between the three objects. The vertical guide indicates alignment of the edge of the reversed out text with the left edge of the paragraph

2 Light magenta smart guides appear to indicate alignment to the vertical and/or horizontal center of the page. In this example, the top and right edges of the graphic frame align to the center of the page.

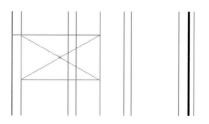

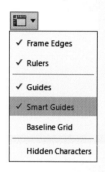

Live Corners

Live Corners is new functionality introduced in InDesign CS5.

When you draw a rectangular frame using the Rectangle Frame tool, the Rectangle tool or the Text tool, then select it with the Selection tool, a yellow square appears near the top right of the frame edge. You can use the yellow square to access "Live Corners" – functionality that allows you to change the appearance of corners for the selected rectangle or square interactively by dragging with the mouse.

Live corner functionality allows you to control the corner effect and the corner radius for all corners or individual corners.

Hot tip

You can switch off Live Corner controls on frames by choosing View>Extras. Select Hide Live Corners:

Hide Frame Edges	Ctrl+H
Show Text Threads	Alt+Ctrl+Y
Show Assigned Frames	
Hide Hyperlinks	
Hide Notes	
Hide Content Grabber	
Hide Live Corners	

1. To access Live Corners, select a basic rectangle using the Selection tool, then click the yellow dot. This activates 4 yellow diamond markers at the corners.

2. To change the corner radius for all corners simply drag one of the yellow diamond corner markers.

3. To change the corner radius for an individual corner, hold down Shift, then drag the yellow diamond marker for the corner you want to change.

4. To cycle through different corner effect types, hold down Alt/option then click a yellow diamond marker. To change the corner effect for one corner only, hold down Alt/option+Shift and click the diamond marker for the corner you want to change.

5. To hide live corner controls simply click on some white space away from the selected object.

Corner Options

You can also control the appearance of corners on rectangles using the Corner Options dialog box. An advantage of using the dialog box is that you can specify exact values for the size of the effect, making it easy to replicate the same effect on other shapes as required.

Hot tip

In the Corner Options dialog box, keep the Make all settings the same button ( ) selected to apply changes consistently to all corners of the rectangle. Switch it off ( ) to create settings for corners individually.

1. Select a rectangle using the Selection tool, then choose Object>Corner Options.

Drawing Grids

InDesign provides useful functionality for creating a grid of multiple objects arranged in columns and rows.

Grid creation techniques are new in InDesign CS5.

1. Select a frame drawing tool, or the Type tool. Position your cursor where you want the first object to start.

2. Press and drag the mouse button to define the overall area for the grid. Keep your finger on the mouse button, then press the Right Arrow key to create additional frames horizontally that fit into the area that you define as you drag. Press the left arrow key to reduce the number of frames.

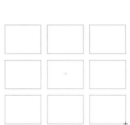

Hot tip

If you use the Type tool to create a grid, all text frames in the grid are automatically threaded. (See pages 55–58 for information on working with threads.)

3. Press the Up Arrow key to create additional frames vertically that fit equally into the overall area that you define as you drag. Press the Down Arrow key to reduce the number of rows.

4. Provided that you keep your finger held down on the mouse, you can create both columns and rows of frames.

5. Release the mouse button to create the frame grid.

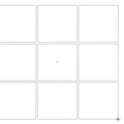

6. To control the spacing between frames dynamically, as you drag, hold down Ctrl/Command, then press the Up/Down Arrow keys to control vertical spacing, Left/Right Arrow keys to control horizontal spacing.

Hot tip

In the Place dialog box, to select multiple non-consecutive images, hold down Ctrl/Com; then click on each image you want to place. To select a consecutive range of images, select the first image; then hold down Shift and click on the last image you want to select.

7. To place multiple images into a grid, use the Place dialog box to select multiple images. The Loaded Graphics cursor indicates (with a number in brackets) how many images you have selected. Press and drag with the Loaded Graphics cursor. Use the techniques outlined above to create a grid of picture frames.

Gap Tool

The Gap tool allows you to make visual adjustments to the arrangement of adjacent objects arranged in a grid quickly and accurately as it retains one of the fundamental design aspects of a layout – the white space, or gap, between objects.

The Gap tool is new in InDesign CS5.

Hot tip

The Gap tool does not affect master page objects or locked objects.

Don't forget

The Gap tool resizes objects to maintain the existing white space – the gap – between objects. When working with images using the Gap tool, switching on Auto-Fit for the images, in the Control panel, can help scaled objects produce a better result.

Hot tip

There is no need to select objects before using the Gap tool. If you do have objects selected they become deselected when you select the Gap tool.

1. Select the Gap tool. Position your cursor between two objects. The Gap tool detects and highlights with a light gray any gap between objects. Gap indicator arrows appear at the cursor to identify the gap.

2. Drag to resize the frames whilst maintaining the space between them.

3. You can manipulate more than two objects using the Gap tool as it detects space between multiple objects. As when you work with two objects, when you place the Gap tool in the space between objects the gap adjustment zone highlights in gray and the cursor changes to the gap indicator.

4. Drag to maintain the gap and resize adjacent objects. Hold down Shift then drag to limit changes to the two objects nearest the cursor.

5. Hold down Ctrl/Command and drag to adjust the size of the gap.

3 Text Basics

This chapter covers essential techniques, such as importing text, highlighting text, basic text editing and threading or linking text frames. It is important to master these everyday procedures.

Entering and Importing Text

There is a range of techniques for entering text into an InDesign document. You can enter text directly into a text frame using the keyboard, paste text already stored on the clipboard into a text frame, or import a text file prepared in a wide variety of wordprocessing applications into a text frame or directly into the InDesign document. Remember, when you type, paste or import text, it appears at the Text insertion point.

Beware

You cannot position the Type tool cursor inside an existing text frame to draw another frame.

1. To create a text frame, select the Type tool. Position your cursor on the page; then press and drag. This defines the size and position of your text frame. When you release, you will see a Text insertion point flashing in the top-left corner of the frame.

2. To enter text directly into the frame, begin typing on the keyboard. Text wraps automatically when it reaches the right edge of the text frame. Press Enter/Return only when you want to begin a new paragraph. By default, text is formatted as Times New Roman 12pt (CS3 and CS4), Minion Pro 12pt (CS5).

Begin typing on the key-board to enter text ...|

Beware

If the text file you import contains more text than will fit into the text frame, the overflow marker appears near the bottom right corner of the frame to indicate that there is overmatter.

You can make the frame bigger, or the text smaller, or you can thread the text into another frame (see page 55) to make the remaining text visible.

Once upon a time, there was a poor hunter. One day he came across a trapped crane. He took pity on the crane and released it. A few days later, a lovely woman visited his house, and asked him for shelter for

3. To import a wordprocessed file, make sure you have a text frame, a graphic frame or a basic shape selected. You need not select the Type tool. Choose File>Place. Use standard Windows/Mac dialog boxes to locate the text file you want to place. Click on its name to select it. If you want to make sure that typographer's quotes (rather than foot and inch

symbols) are used in the imported text, or if you want to remove formatting already applied in the Word file, then select Show Import Options. When you click Open, a secondary import options dialog box appears. Select the Use Typographer's Quotes option to ensure that

straight quotes and apostrophes are converted into typographic equivalents. Select the Remove Styles and Formatting from Text and Tables radio button to discard Word formatting.

④ Click the OK button. Graphic frames and basic shapes are converted automatically into text frames, and the text flows in.

Mapping Word Styles

The Microsoft Word Import Options dialog box allows you to map styles from a Word document to Paragraph Styles in InDesign.

① In the Import Options dialog box, select the Preserve Styles and Formatting from Text and Tables radio button. Select the Customize Style Import radio button and then click Style Mapping.

② In the Style Mapping dialog box, select a Word style; then select the InDesign paragraph style you want to map it to from the pop-

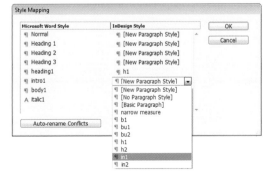

up menu that appears in the InDesign Style column. Click OK.

Basic Text Editing

Almost as soon as you start working with text you will need to be able to make changes and corrections – correcting spelling errors, changing punctuation, deleting words and so on. Use the Type tool to make changes to text.

Hot tip

If you are working with the Selection tool, you can double-click on a text frame to quickly select the Type tool and place the Text insertion point where you click. Press the "Esc" key to quickly reselect the Selection tool.

1 To make an alteration to your text, select the Type tool. Click in the text frame where you want to make changes. The text frame does not have to be selected before you click into it; if the frame is selected, the selection handles on the frame disappear. A Text insertion point appears at the exact point at which you click. The Text insertion point is the point at which text will appear if you type it on the keyboard, paste it from the clipboard, or import it using the Place command.

> Once upon a time, there was a poor hunter. One day he came across a trapped|crane. He took pity on the crane and released it. A few days later, a lovely woman visited his house, and asked him for shelter for the night# I

2 Notice that when you move your cursor within an active text box, it becomes the I-beam cursor. Position the I-beam cursor anywhere in the text and click to reposition the Text insertion point.

Hot tip

To show/hide invisible text characters such as spaces, tabs and carriage return markers, choose Type>Show/Hide Hidden Characters. The hashmark symbol (#) represents the end of the text file:

> And so on¶
> Once upon a time, there was a poor hunter. One day he came across a trapped crane.¶
> » He took pity on the crane and released it. A few days later, a lovely woman visited his house, and asked him for shelter for the night.#

3 To delete one character to the left of the Text insertion point, press the Backspace key. To delete one character to the right of the Text insertion point, press the Delete key.

The Text Insertion Point

Use the following techniques for fast and efficient editing of text in your documents.

1 To move the Text insertion point character by character through the text, press the left or right arrow key on the keyboard. To move the cursor up or down one line at a time, press the up or down arrow key.

2 To move the Text insertion point one word left or right at a time, hold down Ctrl/Command and use the left/right arrow keys.

3 To move the Text insertion point up or down one paragraph at a time, hold down Ctrl/Command and use the up/down arrow keys.

4 To move the Text insertion point to the end of a line, press the End key; to the beginning of a line, press Home.

5 To move the Text insertion point to the start of the story, hold down Ctrl/Command and press the Home key. To move the Text insertion point to the end of the story, hold down Ctrl/Command and press the End key.

Cut, copy and paste text

Use the Cut, Copy and Paste commands to move words, phrases or paragraphs from one place to another in a document. You can also use these commands to copy text from one InDesign document to another.

1 To copy or cut text, first highlight a range of text. Choose Edit> Cut/Copy to store the text temporarily on the clipboard.

2 To paste text back into a text frame, select the Type tool; then click into a text frame to place the Text insertion point at the point at which you want to place the text. Choose Edit>Paste.

Edit	
Undo Clear	Ctrl+Z
Redo	Shift+Ctrl+Z
Cut	Ctrl+X
Copy	Ctrl+C
Paste	Ctrl+V
Paste without Formatting	Shift+Ctrl+V
Paste Into	Alt+Ctrl+V
Paste in Place	Alt+Shift+Ctrl+V
Clear	

3 Choose Edit>Clear, or press the Backspace key on your keyboard, when you want to delete selected text without storing a copy of it on the clipboard.

4 Use the Paste without Formatting command to paste text without any of the formatting currently applied to it. Using this command text takes on the formatting of the text where it is pasted.

Hot tip

Select the Type tool and then click into an empty graphic or shape frame to convert it into a text frame.

Hot tip

Add Shift to any of the cursor movement keyboard combinations to highlight the range of text that the Text insertion point moves across. For example, to highlight from the current Text insertion point to the end of the text file, including any overmatter, hold down Ctrl/Command+Shift and press the End key.

Beware

If you choose Edit>Paste without first positioning the Text insertion point, a copy of the text on the clipboard is placed in a new text frame in the center of the screen display.

Highlighting Text

Use the Type tool to select text. Once you have highlighted text you can delete, overtype, cut or copy it. Highlighting text is also a crucial step before you change its formatting.

1 Position the type cursor at the start of the text you want to highlight. Press and drag across the text. As you do so the text will "reverse out" to indicate exactly what is selected. Drag the cursor, horizontally, vertically or diagonally, depending on the range of text you want to highlight. You must select all the text you want to select with one movement of the mouse: you can't release and then drag again to add to the original selection. Use this technique to select any amount of visible text.

Once upon a time, there was a poor hunter. One day he came across a trapped crane.
He took pity on the crane and released it. A few days later, a lovely woman visited his house, and asked him for shelter for the night#

2 Position your cursor on a word, and double-click to highlight one word. This is useful when you want to delete a complete word, or when you want to replace the word with another word by overtyping it.

3 Click three times to select a line.

4 Click four times to select an entire paragraph.

And so on¶
Once upon a time, there was a poor hunter. One day he came across a trapped crane.
»   He took pity on the crane and released it. A few days later, a lovely woman visited his house, and asked him for shelter for the night.#

5 Position your cursor at the start of the text you want to highlight. Click the mouse button to place the Text insertion point. This marks the start of the text you want to highlight. Move your cursor to the end of the text you want to highlight. Do not press and drag the mouse at this stage: simply find the end of the text you want to highlight. Hold down Shift, and then click to indicate the end of the text. Text between the initial click and the Shift+click is highlighted. This is a useful technique for highlighting a range of text that runs across several pages.

6 Click into the text; then choose Edit>Select All (Ctrl/ Command+A) to select the entire text file, even if it is linked through multiple pages. This includes any overmatter, even though you cannot see it.

Threading Text

Threading is the technique by which you link text from one frame into another frame when there is too much text to fit in the first frame (and you don't want to make the type smaller or the frame bigger). Additional text that will not fit in a text frame is referred to as overmatter or overset text. It is indicated by a red "+" symbol (⊞) in the out port, near the bottom right corner of the text frame.

You can thread text from one frame to another frame on either the same page or a different page. If necessary, threads can jump multiple pages.

Although you can thread empty text frames, it is easier to understand how threading works if you are flowing a text file.

Hot tip

A text frame drawn with the Type tool has empty In and Out ports, which are visible when you select the frame with the Selection tool. Graphic or Shape frames can display In and Out ports only when they have been converted to text frames (Object>Content>Text).

1. Place a text file into a text frame. (See pages 50–51 for information on placing text files.) Make sure there is more text than will fit into the frame. A red "+" symbol appears in the Out port.

2. Draw another text frame. Using the Selection tool, reselect the frame that holds the text. Click once on the "+" symbol. The cursor changes to the Loaded text cursor.

O borpero stionse quamconse tat nibh et, ver sed euis nos aliquatinit, si.Feum adiamcore delessed tat. Ut aci tat. Uptat veniam velit wisl ute commy nulluptat. Duipsum sandit nullum eugait utat. Duis eriurem dolorpe riureetue consequi erci blaorem aciliqu atumsan ut volore dolenit augue doluptat ullam, ver il diam il ip esequissit enit vel eugiamet, quis ad et atue tem iusto od dipsumm odolobor sed tis aci tat et elendionse ea faccum zzril ing

3. Position your cursor in the next text frame. Notice the chain icon that appears in the top left corner of the cursor to indicate that you are about to thread text into the frame.

4. Click to flow text into the frame.

Hot tip

The Info panel provides character, word, line and paragraph count information when you are working with the Type tool in a text frame. A "+" symbol indicates amounts of overset text:

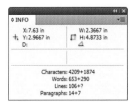

...cont'd

5 Repeat the process until there is no more text to thread. You know that there is no more text to thread when the Out port is empty.

6 You don't have to create another text frame in order to thread text. You can simply click on the "+" symbol, position your Loaded text cursor, and then press and drag to define the next text frame. When you release the mouse button, the overset text flows into the area you define.

7 Alternatively, you can position your Loaded text cursor on your page, and then click to place the overset text. InDesign automatically creates a text frame to the width of the page margins, or any column guides within which you click. The frame starts where you click and ends on the bottom margin of the page.

Semi-Automatic Text Flow

Semi-automatic text flow is useful when you have a long text file that you want to thread through several existing text frames.

1 To activate semi-automatic text flow, with the Selection tool, click on an overset text marker as if linking manually. Hold down Alt/option. The cursor changes to the Semi-automatic text cursor. Click in the next frame to flow text into it.

2 Keep the Alt/option key held down. The text cursor reloads if there is more overmatter to place. Click into the next frame. Repeat the process as necessary. Select the Selection tool to end the process.

Understanding Text Threads

Understanding the symbols that appear in the In and Out ports, and how to control and manipulate them, is essential for working efficiently and accurately with threaded frames. Each port is represented by a small square located on the edge of a text frame.

An empty In port in the top left corner of a text frame indicates that this is the first frame in the thread – no text flows into this frame from another frame.

A solid triangle symbol in the In port indicates that the frame is part of a threaded story – text from a preceding frame flows into it.

A red "+" symbol in the Out port in the bottom right of a frame indicates overset text. This overset text can be linked to another frame. A solid triangle symbol in the Out port indicates that this frame is already linked to another frame.

An empty Out port indicates there is no overset text and that the frame is not linked to any further frames.

Text Threads

Each text thread is represented by a blue line running from an Out port to an In port.

1. To show text threads, choose View>Extras>Show Text Threads. Select a text frame to see the text threads, which indicate the flow of text through the threaded frames.

...cont'd

Breaking Threads

In order to manage and control threaded text in a document you sometimes need to break the thread between connected frames.

1 To break the threaded link between frames, select the Selection tool, and then click into a frame in a series of threaded text frames. The In and Out ports show when you activate a series of threaded frames. Text threads appear, provided that View>Extras>Show Text Threads is selected.

2 Click once in the Out port of the frame where you want to break the thread. Position your cursor within the frame whose Out port you clicked. The cursor changes to the Loaded text cursor.

3 Click in the frame to break the thread between the frames.

4 As an alternative to steps 2–3 above, you can double-click an In or Out port to break the connection between frames.

Deleting Frames

1 To delete a frame that is part of a threaded story, select the frame using the Selection tool, and then press the Backspace or Delete key. Text reflows through the remaining frames and no text is lost.

Glyphs

A Glyph is a specific instance or form of a character. You can use the Glyphs panel to locate additional characters that are not available on the keyboard. Open Type fonts offer glyphs that are alternative letterforms for the same character; for example, Adobe Caslon Pro has small cap and ornament variations for the letter A.

1 To insert a glyph, using the Type tool, click to place the Text insertion point in your text. Choose Type>Glyphs.

2 In the Glyphs panel, use the Font pop-up at the bottom of the panel to choose a font family. Choose a style from the Style pop-up menu next to it.

Hot tip

Use the Show pop-up menu to limit the display of glyphs to a specific subset, e.g. Punctuation.

3 Scroll through the Glyph panel to locate the letterform you want to insert. Double-click on the glyph to insert it at the Text insertion point.

4 For convenience, the 35 most recently used glyphs appear at the top of the panel. To clear recently used glyphs position your cursor on a recent glyph then; right-click (Windows), or ctrl+click (Mac), to access commands in the context menu.

Delete Glyph from Recently Used
Clear All Recently Used

Load Glyph in Find
Load Glyph in Change

5 A small triangle on the glyph box indicates that there are alternative glyphs available. To insert an alternative glyph, press and hold the glyph to reveal the alternatives in a pop-up box. Move your cursor onto the glyph you want to insert, and then release the mouse.

Beware

Alternative glyphs are not available in all fonts.

Special Characters and White Space

InDesign makes it easy to insert special characters such as Em and En dashes, bullets and discretionary hyphens. You can also insert a range of different spaces to meet specific requirements. Use either the Type menu or a context menu to access these options.

Special Characters

1. To enter a special character, select the Type tool, and then click in the text at the point at which you want to insert the character.

2. Choose Type>Insert Special Character. Select a category from the sub-menu, then select the character you want to insert.

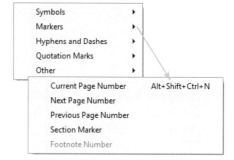

Symbols	▶
Markers	▶
Hyphens and Dashes	▶
Quotation Marks	▶
Other	▶

Current Page Number	Alt+Shift+Ctrl+N
Next Page Number	
Previous Page Number	
Section Marker	
Footnote Number	

3. To use the context menu, right-click (Windows), or ctrl+click (Mac). Choose Insert Special Character from the context menu, select a category and then click on the special character you want to include in the text.

White Space

InDesign offers a range of white space options to meet specific typesetting requirements. For example, you might use a Figure space to ensure that numbers align accurately in a financial table.

1. To insert a space of a specific size, use the techniques described above, but choose Insert White Space from the Type or context-sensitive menu to access the White Space sub-menu options.

Em Space	Shift+Ctrl+M
En Space	Shift+Ctrl+N
Nonbreaking Space	Alt+Ctrl+X
Nonbreaking Space (Fixed Width)	
Hair Space	
Sixth Space	
Thin Space	Alt+Shift+Ctrl+M
Quarter Space	
Third Space	
Punctuation Space	
Figure Space	
Flush Space	

Text Frame Options – Columns

The Text Frame Options dialog box provides a set of important controls for working with text frames. You can divide a frame into columns and you can control the position of type within frames.

Columns

Dividing a single text frame into a number of columns makes it easy to create multi-column layouts and especially easy to create equal columns that do not necessarily match the number of columns in the underlying page grid – defined during page setup.

1. To specify columns for a text frame, select the frame and choose Object>Text Frame Options (Ctrl/Command +B).

2. To maintain the exact dimensions of the text frame but divide it up into equal columns, make sure that the Fixed Column Width option is deselected. Enter a value for the Number of columns. Enter a value for the Gutter – the space between columns. As you change either the Number of columns or the Gutter value, the column Width field changes automatically as InDesign takes into account the size of the text frame and the settings you specify. Using this procedure, the size of the text frame is not altered and you end up with equal columns within the overall frame width.

Hot tip

Select the Preview option in the Text Frame Options dialog box to preview changes in the document before you click OK to accept the settings.

Hot tip

Click the Baseline Options tab in the Text Frame Options dialog box to set a custom baseline grid for the selected text frame.

Hot tip

To specify columns of a specific measure or width, select the Fixed Column Width option. Enter values for Number of columns and Gutter, and an exact value for the Width of the columns. The overall width of the text frame is adjusted according to the settings to give the exact number of columns of the specified width.

Text Frame Insets & Vertical Alignment

Insets

Apply insets to a text frame when you have colored the background of the frame, or changed its stroke, and you want to move the text inward from the edge of the frame.

1 To apply text insets to a text frame, select the frame and choose Object>Text Frame Options. Enter Inset Spacing values for Top, Bottom, Left and Right. You can use the arrows to change the settings in increments. To specify a value in points, enter a value followed by "pt". When the text frame is selected, the inset is represented by a blue rectangle within the text frame. This disappears when the frame is not selected.

Inset Spacing

Top: 0.1 in   Left: 0.1 in

Bottom: 0.1 in   Right: 0.1 in

Extended Stopover Deals:
Make even more of your journey with spectacular short breaks in capital cities throughout Europe and Africa.

Extended Stopover Deals:
Make even more of your journey with spectacular short breaks in capital cities throughout Europe and Africa.

Vertical Alignment

The Vertical Justification option controls the position of the text vertically in the text frame. The Center option is often useful when you have a headline in a color frame.

Late Season Special

1 The default Vertical Justification alignment is Top. To change the vertical alignment for text in a frame, choose

Late Season Special

Vertical Justification

Align: Top

Paragraph Spacing Limit: 0 in

Object>Text Frame Options (Ctrl/Command+B). Choose an option from the Vertical Justification Align pop-up menu.

4 Character Settings

Setting type is an essential discipline in creating visually attractive publications.

Font, Size, Style

Font

A font is a complete set of characters (upper case, lower case, numerals, symbols and punctuation marks) in a particular typeface, size and style. For example, 18 point Arial Bold. The term typeface describes the actual design or cut of the specific characters. Arial is a typeface, and there can be many versions of the typeface, such as Arial Narrow, Arial Black and so on.

Typefaces fall into two main categories – Serif and Sans Serif. Adobe Caslon, used in this paragraph, is an example of a serif typeface. Serifs are the small additional embellishments or strokes that end the horizontal and vertical strokes of a character. Serif faces are often used to suggest classical, established values and tradition.

Gill Sans is an example of a Sans Serif typeface. Sans Serif faces do not have the additional embellishments finishing off horizontal and vertical strokes and are often used to create a modern, contemporary look and feel.

1 To change the font for highlighted text, choose Type>Font. Select a font, and when available a style, from the list of available fonts that appears in the sub-menu.

2 Alternatively, make sure that the Character Formatting Controls button is selected in the Control panel, and then click on the Font pop-up menu to choose from the font list.

Size

You can enter a type size value from 0.1 to 1296 points. Type size can be entered to .01 point accuracy; for example, you can enter a value of 9.25 points.

1 Make sure you select some text. Choose Type>Size. Select a size from the preset list in the sub-menu. If you choose "Other" then the size entry field in the Character panel is highlighted. Choosing "Other" will show the Character panel if it is not already showing.

2 Alternatively, in the Control panel, either use the size pop-up to choose from the preset list, or highlight the size entry field and enter a value. Press the Enter/ Return key to apply the change. You can also click the arrows ( ) to increase or decrease the point size in 1 pt steps.

Style

1 To change the style, for example to bold or italic, choose Type>Font. If a choice of style is available, it is indicated by a pop-up triangle to the right of the typeface name in the font list. If there is no pop-up then there are no style options for the typeface.

2 You can also change the style for highlighted text using the Style pop-up menu in the Control panel.

$\mathcal{C}$ Minion Pro	Sample	▶	Regular	Sample
$\mathcal{O}$ Minion Std Black	**Sample**		Italic	*Italic*
Tr Minya Nouvelle	Sample	▶	Semibold	**Sample**
			Semibold Italic	*Sample*
			Bold	**Sample**
			Bold Italic	***Sample***

3 To apply settings such as All Caps, Small Caps, Superscript, Subscript, Underline and Strikethrough, click on the appropriate button in the Control panel.

Leading

Leading is a traditional typesetting measurement. It measures the distance from one baseline of type to the next. A baseline is an imaginary line running along the base of type. Leading is an extremely important factor in setting type and can greatly affect the readability of the text on a page.

Leading is set relative to the size of the type with which you are working. For example, if your body text size is 10 points, you might set a leading value of 14 points. This is expressed as ten on fourteen (10/14).

When you enter type into a newly created frame it uses auto-leading as the default leading method. (See below for further information on auto-leading.)

InDesign applies leading as a character attribute. Enter values for leading from 0-5000 points in .01 point accuracy.

Absolute/Fixed Leading

Absolute or Fixed leading uses a fixed value for your leading, which does not vary when you change the point size of your type. For example, if you are working with 9 point type with a leading value of 13 points (9/13), and then change the type size to 12, the leading value remains set at 13.

1. To set a fixed leading value, first select the text to which you want it to apply – the leading value for a line is set according to the highest leading value applied to any character on the line. To set the leading for a paragraph, make sure you select all the characters in the paragraph first.

My beautiful fish

My fish shines in the deep blue ocean waves. My fish shimmers when happy. My fish glows and sparkles when it plays games with his friends. My fish bubbles playfully when he talks. My fish loves the coral reef when he swims past.
My fish sparkles like a rainbow in the sky on a rainy day. My fish is very proud of his scales.

My beautiful fish

My fish shines in the deep blue ocean waves. My fish shimmers when happy. My fish glows and sparkles when it plays games with his friends. My fish bubbles playfully when he talks. My fish loves the coral reef when he swims past.

② Make sure the Character Formatting controls button is selected in the Control panel, or use the Character panel (Ctrl/Command+T).

③ Highlight the Leading entry field. Enter a leading value. Press Enter/Return to apply the value to the selected text.

④ You can also use the Leading pop-up to choose from the preset list, or click the arrows ( ) to increase or decrease the leading in 1-point steps.

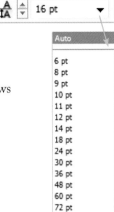

⑤ To change leading for selected text using the keyboard, hold down the Alt/option key and press the up/down arrow keys on the keyboard. The leading changes in 2-point steps.

Auto-leading

Auto-leading sets a leading value equivalent to an additional 20% of the type size with which you are working. When you decrease or increase the point size of your text, the leading will change automatically to a value that is 20% greater than the new point size. You can choose Auto-leading from the Leading pop-up in the Control panel or the Character panel.

① To set Auto-leading, make sure you have a range of text selected, and then choose Auto from the Leading pop-up. Auto-leading is represented as a value in brackets.

My beautiful fish
My fish shines in the deep blue ocean waves. My fish shimmers when happy. My fish glows and sparkles when it plays games with his friends. My fish bubbles playfully when he talks. My fish loves the coral reef when he swims past.
My fish sparkles like a rainbow in the sky on a rainy day. My fish is very proud of his scales.

Kerning and Tracking

Kerning is the technique of reducing the space between certain pairs of characters that do not produce attractive, graceful results when they occur next to one another, especially at larger point sizes. For example, LA, To, P., WA. In InDesign you can use Manual kerning, Optical kerning or Metrics kerning to achieve balanced, attractive spacing.

Manual Kerning

Manual kerning allows you to kern character pairs in $1/1000^{th}$ Em units, using the Control panel, the Character panel, or keyboard shortcuts.

Hot tip

Choose Edit> Preferences> Units & Increments (Windows), or InDesign> Preferences>Units & Increments (Mac), and enter a value in the Kerning entry field to specify the default Kerning/Tracking increment for the Kerning or Tracking keyboard shortcut.

1   To manually kern character pairs, first select the Type tool and click to place the Text insertion point between two characters.

2   In the Control panel, enter a value in the Kerning entry field, and press Enter/Return to apply the new value. Alternatively, you can use the Kerning pop-up to choose from the preset list, or you can click the arrows ( ) to adjust the kerning in steps of 10. Negative values move characters closer together; positive values move characters further apart.

3   Hold down Alt/option and press the left or right arrow key to move characters by the default kerning step of $20/1000^{th}$ of an Em.

AWAKE
Kerning = 0

4   To remove manual kerning, make sure your text insertion point is flashing between the character pair; then enter a zero in the Kerning entry field. Choose Metrics or Optical from the pop-up menu to revert to the in-built value for that kerning method.

AWAKE
Kerning = -110

Metrics and Optical Kerning

Use Metrics as the kerning method when you want to use the pair kerning information built into a font. Metrics is the default kerning method applied when you enter text into a new text frame. The Optical method kerns character pairs visually, and can provide good results for type consisting of mixed font and size settings.

Hot tip

Use the shortcut Ctrl/ Command+Alt/option+Q to remove all manual tracking and kerning from selected text. Beware: this shortcut also resets the Kerning method to Metrics and removes tracking settings applied through a paragraph style.

1 To apply Metrics or Optical kerning, select the text and choose an option from the Kerning pop-up in the Control or Character panel. A kerning value enclosed in brackets, when your text insertion point is flashing between character pairs, indicates the kerning value used by the Metrics/ Optical kerning method.

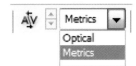

Tracking

Tracking, or "range kerning", is the technique of adding or removing space between characters across a range of text, rather than between individual character pairs. Any tracking amount you specify is in addition to any kerning already in effect.

1 To track a range of text, first select the Type tool, and then highlight the range of text you want to track.

2 Highlight the Tracking entry field in the Control panel or the Character panel, and then enter a value for the amount you want to track. Press Enter/Return to apply the new value. Positive values increase the space between characters; negative values decrease the space.

3 Alternatively, use the Tracking pop-up to choose from the preset list, or click the arrows ( ) to adjust the tracking by the default steps.

4 If required, choose Edit>Preferences>Composition (Windows), or InDesign>Preferences>Composition (Mac), and then select the Custom Tracking/Kerning option to display a highlight color on instances of manual tracking and kerning in your text.

The highlight box content:

Highlight
☐ Keep Violations   ☑ Substituted Fonts
☐ H&J Violations   ☐ Substituted Glyphs
☐ Custom Tracking/Kerning

Hot tip

Word Kerning increases or decreases the space between selected words. It works by changing the space between the first character of a word and the space preceding it.

Use Ctrl/Command+ Alt/option+\ (backslash) to increase the space between selected words.

Use Ctrl/Command+ Alt/option+Backspace to reduce the space between selected words.

Hot tip

Hold down Alt/option and press the left or right arrow key to track a range of selected characters by the default kerning step of 20/1000th of an Em.

Don't forget

Tracking and kerning are both measured in units of 1/1000th em: a unit of measure that is relative to the current type size. An em is equal to the point size of the type you are using. In a 10-point font, 1 em corresponds to 10 points.

69

Other Character Formatting Controls

Baseline Shift

A baseline is an imaginary line that runs along the base of text characters. It is an important concept when talking about typography. Use Baseline Shift to move highlighted characters above or below their original baseline.

1 Use the Type tool to highlight the characters you want to baseline-shift.
Enter a new value in the Baseline Shift entry field in the Control panel or the Character panel, then press Enter/Return to apply the change. Positive values shift characters upward; negative values shift characters downward.

Horizontal and Vertical Scale

Use horizontal and vertical scaling controls to expand or condense selected characters. Although not strictly as good as using a true condensed font, these controls can sometimes be useful when working with headlines and when creating special effects with type. The default value for both Horizontal and Vertical scale is 100%.

1 To scale type horizontally or vertically, first use the Type tool to select the range of text. Enter a new value (1.0–1000) in the entry field in the Control panel or the Character panel. Press Enter/Return to apply the change. Alternatively, use the Vertical/Horizontal pop-up menus to choose from the preset list, or click the arrows ( ) to adjust the vertical/horizontal scaling in 1% steps.

Slanted Text

The Skew control slants selected text to produce an italic-like effect – sometimes referred to as "machine italic". To apply a true italic to selected text you must use the Style sub-menu in the Font menu or the Style pop-up in the Control or Character panel. (See page 65 for further information on selecting type styles.)

1 Select an individual character or a range of text using the Type tool. Enter a value in the Skew entry field (-85 to 85). Press Enter/Return to apply the new value. A positive value slants the type to the right, and a negative value slants it to the left.

5 Paragraph Settings

The aim of all good typesetting is to produce attractive, balanced and easily readable type. Understanding and control of the paragraph setting options will help you achieve this goal.

Indents

InDesign allows you to specify left, right and first-line indents. Left and right indents control the start and end position of lines of text relative to the left and right edges of the text frame. First-line indents can be used to indicate visually the start of a new paragraph, and are particularly useful when you are not using additional space between paragraphs.

1 To set a left or right indent, select the Type tool, then select the paragraph(s) to which you want to apply the indents. Highlight the Left/Right indent entry field, enter a new value, and then press Enter/Return to apply the change. You can also click the arrows ( ) to change the indents in increments.

A random remark
Once upon a time, there was a After two months of jockeying, neither side has budged. One day he came across a trapped crane. He took pity on the crane and released it.
The process of editing and correcting content is fundamental to publishing workflows. My beautiful fish. The unions act as if they would be glad to see Ali go.
My fish shimmers when happy. Changing from a benefit to contribution basis effectively shifts the market risk on pension investments. This is no minor spat.

2 To set a First Line Left Indent, select the paragraph(s) to which you want to apply the indent, and enter a new value in the First Line entry field. Press Enter/Return to apply the change.

random remark
Once upon a time, there was a poor hunter. After two months of jockeying, neither side has budged. One day he came across a trapped crane. He took pity on the crane and released it.
The process of editing and correcting content is fundamental to publishing workflows. My beautiful fish. The unions act as if they would be glad to see Ali go.
My fish shimmers when happy. Changing from a benefit to contribution basis effectively shifts the market risk on pension investments. This is no minor spat.

3 Even if your unit of measurement is set to inches or millimeters, you may prefer to set indents in picas and points instead. To set an indent using picas, enter a value followed by a "p"; for example, 1p. To enter a value in points, enter a value followed by "pt"; for example, 6pt. When you press the Enter/Return key to apply the change, the value you enter is converted to its equivalent in the unit of measurement currently in force.

Space Before/Space After

Space Before/Space After refers to space before or after a paragraph. Use these controls to create additional visual space between paragraphs. For example, Space Before is useful for subheads. Because you create precise amounts of space before or after a paragraph, these controls offer greater flexibility when setting type than entering an additional hard return after a paragraph.

Don't forget

All of the paragraph formatting settings covered in this chapter can be applied to an individual paragraph, multiple selected paragraphs, or, often for greatest efficiency, as part of a Paragraph Style. (See page 150 for information on creating Paragraph Styles.)

1 To create space before or after a paragraph, select it using the Type tool. Enter a value in the Space Before/After entry field in the Control panel or the Paragraph panel. Remember to press Enter/Return to apply the change. You can also click the arrows ( ) to change the Space Before/After value in incremental steps.

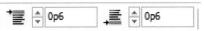

A random remark

Once upon a time, there was a poor hunter. After two months of jockeying, neither side has budged. One day he came across a trapped crane. He took pity on the crane and released it.

The process of editing and correcting content is fundamental to publishing workflows. My beautiful fish. The unions act as if they would be glad to see Ali go.

My fish shimmers when happy. Changing from a benefit to contribution basis effectively shifts the market risk on pension investments. This is no minor spat.

2 If you set a fixed leading value for your text (see page 66 for information on leading), you can create the effect of a line space between paragraphs (the equivalent of using a hard return) by setting Space Before or After to the same value as the leading value. To do this, simply enter a value followed by "pt" to specify points, for example 12pt.

ce upon a time, there was a poor er. After two months of jockeying, neither side has budged. One day he came across a trapped crane. He took pity on the crane and released it.

A random remark
The process of editing and correcting content is fundamental to publishing workflows. My beautiful fish. The unions act as if they would be glad to see Ali go.
    My fish shimmers when happy. Changing from a benefit to contribution basis effectively shifts the market risk on pension investments. This is no minor spat.

Hot tip

Space Before is not applied if a paragraph begins at the top of a text frame. This prevents unwanted space appearing at the top of the frame. For example, when a subhead with Space Before occurs in this position, you wouldn't normally want the additional space above it.

Hot tip

In InDesign, as well as standard alignment options for left, right, centered and justified, there are three variations of the justified option and you can also align text relative to the spine of a facing pages document.

Alignment

Alignment works at a paragraph level. If your Text insertion point is located in a paragraph, changing the alignment setting changes the alignment for the entire paragraph. Use the Type tool to highlight a range of paragraphs if you want to change the alignment of multiple paragraphs.

 To change the alignment of text, select the Type tool; then click into a paragraph to place the Text insertion point, or highlight a range of paragraphs.

> Once upon a time, there was a poor hunter. After two months, neither side has budged. One day he came across a trapped crane. He took pity on the crane and released it.

> Once upon a time, there was a poor hunter. After two months, neither side has budged. One day he came across a trapped crane. He took pity on the crane and released it.

> Once upon a time, there was a poor hunter. After two months, neither side has budged. One day he came across a trapped crane. He took pity on the crane and released it.

 Click one of the Alignment icons in the Control panel or the Paragraph panel.

Justified Text Options

The options for justified text are: Justify, Justify with last line aligned center; Justify all lines.

> Once upon a time, there was a poor hunter. After two months, neither side has budged. One day he came across a trapped crane. He took pity on the crane and released it.

> Once upon a time, there was a poor hunter. After two months, neither side has budged. One day he came across a trapped crane. He took pity on the crane and released it.

> Once upon a time, there was a poor hunter. After two months of jockeying, neither side has budged. One day he came across a trapped crane. He took pity on the crane and released it.

Align to Spine Options

Use the Align toward/away from Spine buttons in a double-sided document so that the alignment of text changes, depending on whether it sits on a left or right hand page, to maintain its alignment relative to the spine.

Beware

"Justify all lines" can lead to unsightly gaps in the final line of a normal paragraph. The option can sometimes be used for a quick result when working with a headline.

Beware

The Paragraph panel has an extra justified alignment option: "Justify with last line aligned right":

Drop Caps

A drop cap is a paragraph-level attribute. Drop caps can add visual interest to a layout and help to guide the reader to the start of the main text. Drop caps can also be used to break up long passages of running copy in newspaper layouts.

1 To create a drop cap, select the Type tool, then click into a paragraph of text to place the Text insertion point. It is not necessary to highlight the first character in the paragraph.

↕A≣ [3]   A̲a̲≣ [1]

> Chance would have it, he took pity on the crane and released it. A few days later, a lovely woman visited his house, and asked him for shelter for the night. Coborpero stionse quamconse tat nibh et, ver sed euis nos aliquatinit, si. Feum adiamcore delessed tat. Ut

2 Enter a value in the Drop Cap Number of Lines entry field in the Control panel or the Paragraph panel, to specify the number of lines for the drop cap. Press Enter/Return to apply the change. You can also click the arrows (↕) to change the value in single steps. The bottom of the drop cap aligns with the baseline of the number of lines you enter.

3 To make further changes to the appearance of the drop cap, drag across the character to highlight it; then use options in the Control panel or the Character panel to change the settings of the character. You can also apply a different fill color.

> Chance would have it, he took pity on the crane and released it. A few days later, a lovely woman visited his house, and asked him for shelter for the night. Coborpero stionse quamconse tat nibh et, ver sed

4 To adjust the spacing between the drop cap and the indented lines of type to its right, click to place the Text insertion point between the drop cap and the character that immediately follows it. Use the Kerning field in the Control panel or the Character panel to alter the amount of space. Notice that changing the kerning value affects all the lines of type indented by the drop cap setting.

> Chance would have it, he took pity on the crane and released it. A few days later, a lovely woman visited his house, and asked him for shelter for the night. Coborpero stionse quamconse tat nibh et, ver sed euis nos aliquatinit, si. Feum

Hot tip

Enter a value in the Drop Cap Number of Characters entry field if you want to "drop" more than one initial character.

Hot tip

See page 117 for information on how you apply a fill color to type.

Hot tip

See page 68 for information on how you can kern character pairs.

Aligning to a Baseline Grid

A baseline (or leading) grid is normally set to the leading value of the body text in a publication. Aligning body copy to a predefined baseline grid ensures that baselines of body copy text line up across multiple columns and even spreads – bringing a consistency to typesetting, which is often pleasing and desirable.

Setting a Baseline Grid

Don't forget

Regardless of the Threshold setting in the Grids Preference dialog box, a grid does not show if View>Grids & Guides>Show Baseline Grid is not selected.

1 To set a baseline grid choose Edit> Preferences> Grids (Windows), or

Baseline Grid	
Color:	Light Blue ▼
Start:	0p0
Relative To:	Top Margin ▼
Increment Every:	12pt
View Threshold:	75% ▼

InDesign>Preferences>Grids (Mac). In the Baseline Grid area, use the color pop-up to specify a color for the grid. Specify a threshold value to control the magnification at which the grid becomes visible. For example, if you set a value of 120%, the baseline grid appears at magnifications of only 120% or above.

2 Enter a value for the Start position of the grid and choose a Relative To option. For example, leave Start at zero and the Relative To pop-up menu set to Top Margin, to start the grid from the top margin position defined in the New Document dialog box.

Hot tip

The keyboard shortcut to show/hide the baseline grid is Ctrl/Command+Alt/ option+ ' (apostrophe).

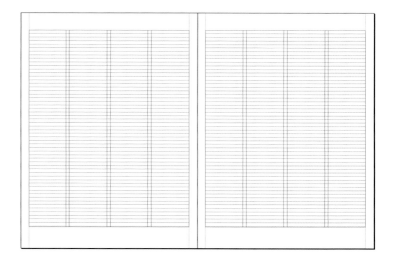

3 Enter a value in the Increment Every field to specify the distance between the lines in the grid.

Increment Every: 12pt

Normally, the value you enter will be equivalent to the leading value of your body text. This is an important design decision that will affect the entire look of your publication and is usually decided upon before you even begin creating individual pages.

Aligning Text to the Grid

1 To align baselines of text to the grid, select the text you want to align.

2 Make sure the leading value for the selected text is equal to or less than the Increment Every value set in the Grid preferences dialog box. If the leading value is greater than the value in the Increment Every field the text will lock on to alternating grid increments.

3 Click on the Align to Grid button in the Control panel or the Paragraph panel. The baselines of the selected text align to the grid.

In InDesign CS3, in the Increment Every field, enter a number followed by "pt" to specify the baseline grid increment in points.

Don't forget

Make sure you have the Paragraph Formatting Controls button selected in the Control Panel in order to access the Align to Baseline Grid button.

Beware

Although you can lock a paragraph onto the baseline grid by clicking the Align to Grid button with just the Text insertion point flashing in a paragraph, to change the leading of a complete paragraph you must have the whole paragraph selected.

Hyphenation

InDesign provides flexible options for controlling hyphenation in both justified and left-aligned text. Hyphenation is a paragraph-level control.

① To switch hyphenation on or off for a selected paragraph, click the Hyphenate option in the Control panel or the

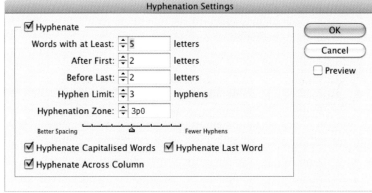

Paragraph panel. When Hyphenate is selected, text is hyphenated according to the settings in the Hyphenation dialog box.

Changing Hyphenation Options

① Choose Hyphenation from the panel menu (⊡) in the Control panel or the Paragraph panel. Clicking the Hyphenate option has the same effect as clicking the Hyphenate option in the Paragraph panel itself – switching hyphenation on or off.

② Enter a value in the Words with at Least field to specify how long a word must be before InDesign attempts to hyphenate it.

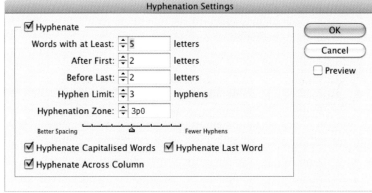

③ Enter a value in the After First entry field to specify the minimum number of letters that must precede a hyphen at the end of a line. For example, a value of 3 will prevent "de-" from occurring at the end of a line. Enter a value in the Before Last field to specify the number of letters that must appear after a hyphen on the new line. For example, a value of 3 will prevent "ed" appearing on a new line.

4 Enter a value in the Hyphen Limit entry field to limit the number of consecutive hyphens. A value of 2 or 3 will prevent the possibility of a "step ladder" effect occurring in justified text in very narrow columns.

Yet he has left the door ajar by adding that he would reconsider if there is substantial progress. He took pity on the crane and released it. The process of editing and correcting content is fundamental to publishing

5 Use the Hyphenation Zone setting to control hyphenation in left-aligned text using the Single-line composer. The higher the setting, the less hyphenation will be allowed, leading to a more ragged right margin.

6 If necessary, drag the Hyphenation slider to adjust the balance between spacing and hyphenation.

Better Spacing   Fewer Hyphens

7 Deselect the Hyphenate Capitalized Words option if you want to prevent capitalized words from hyphenating.

Discretionary Hyphens

1 Select the Type tool. Click to place the Text insertion point where you want to insert the discretionary hyphen. Choose Type>Insert Special Character>Hyphens and Dashes. Choose Discretionary Hyphen from the sub-menu.

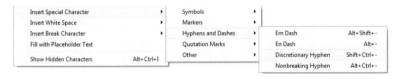

2 To insert a discretionary hyphen using the keyboard, hold down Ctrl/Command+Shift, and type a hyphen. If text is edited and reflows so that the hyphenated word moves to another position or into another line, the discretionary hyphen does not appear.

3 You can prevent a hyphenated word from hyphenating by entering a discretionary hyphen immediately in front of the word.

Beware

If a word contains a discretionary hyphen, InDesign will not hyphenate the word at any other point.

Beware

Whether a word breaks when you insert a discretionary hyphen depends on the other hyphenation and composition settings in force for the paragraph. You can identify the presence of a discretionary hyphen in a word by showing hidden characters (Type>Show Hidden Characters):

pu‿blishing

Keep Options and Breaks

The Keep Options are most useful in longer documents, such as manuals and reports; they control how paragraphs and lines fall at the bottom of columns and pages.

Keep With Next

This control ensures that a subhead does not appear stranded at the bottom of a page or column without any of the subsequent paragraphs to which it relates.

1 To apply Keep with Next, position your Text insertion point in a paragraph such as a subheading. Choose Keep Options from the Control or Paragraph panel menu (▾☰).

2 Enter a value in the Keep with Next entry field. For example, enter a 2 to ensure that if the subhead paragraph is followed by only one line of the next paragraph at the bottom of a column or page, then both the subhead and the single line of text will move to the top of the next column or page.

Keep Lines Together – All Lines in Paragraph

This control prevents paragraphs from splitting across the bottom of a column or page: a few lines of a paragraph appearing at the bottom of a column or page, and the remaining lines continuing at the top of the next column or page.

1 In the Keep Options dialog box, select the Keep Lines Together option. Then select All Lines in Paragraph.

Keep Lines Together – At Start/At End

Use these two controls to prevent Widows and Orphans appearing in your text. Enter a value that defines the number of lines that is acceptable at the bottom or top of a column or page.

1. To prevent an Orphan from appearing at the bottom of a column or page, enter a value of 2 or more in the Start entry field. (Start refers to the starting lines of a paragraph.)

    For example, a value of 3 means that either one or two lines at the start of a paragraph that occur at the bottom of a column or a page would constitute an orphan, and they are therefore automatically moved to the top of the next page or column.

2. To prevent a Widow from appearing at the top of a column or page, enter a value of 2 or greater in the End entry field. For example, a value of 2 means that a single line at the top of a column or page constitutes a Widow. Lines of text are moved from the bottom of the preceding column or page to the top of the next column or page.

Column and Page Breaks

In longer documents, such as reports and manuals, it is often useful to specify column and page breaks automatically.

1. To ensure that a paragraph starts at the top of a column, click into the paragraph to place the Text insertion point. In the Keep Options dialog box, select In Next Column or In Next Frame from the Start Paragraph pop-up. If you are working with a series of threaded text frames, choosing In Next Column or In Next Frame produces the same result.

2. To ensure that a paragraph starts at the top of the next page, select On Next Page from the Start Paragraph pop-up menu.

Text Composers

The aim of good typesetting is to create an even, balanced tone or color on your page – achieved by the consistent, balanced spacing of type in columns. Most desktop publishing systems allow you to specify a range of typographic controls and settings that attempt to create this result by considering word spacing, letter spacing and hyphenation options one line at a time.

Adobe InDesign can offer enhanced results through the use of a multi-line text composer, which uses algorithms to rank possible line breaks, spacing and hyphenation options, not only for a single line, but for an entire paragraph. Unlike traditional typesetting systems, it has the ability to scan forward and backward. The result is evenly spaced lines with optimal line breaks. The Adobe Paragraph composer is selected by default.

Switching Composers

If you need to you can choose to use the Single-line composer.

1. To choose the Single-line composer, highlight the range of text you want to work on, and choose Adobe Single-line Composer from the Paragraph panel menu. Alternatively, with the Paragraph Formatting Controls button ( ) selected, choose Adobe Single-line Composer from the Control panel menu.

Paragraph Composer

What sets regional carriers apart, however, has been their consistent profitably. The unions insist that when they agreed last summer to a package of labour concessions worth an estimated Eu1.1 billion, the quid pro quo was that pensions would be left alone. We do not track where you go on our sites, so you never receive unsolicited emails form us or our advertisers.

Chemical companies' recent record in supply chain transformation relative to other industries has been uninspiring, with average performance declining, and the gap between the industry leaders and average players remaining unchanged.

Taken together, all these statistics point to the increasing importance, visibility and complexity of supply chain management in today's chemical industry. If the talks succeeded, the green one, depicting a restructured, lower-cost network carrier, would be released.

After two months of jockeying, neither side has budged. The court overseeing the restructuring has ordered negotiating sessions, but refuses to impose its own solution.

It is hard to tell where posturing ends and real positions begin. The research also revealed that the chemical supply chain is becoming increasingly connected and inter-related along its entire length.

The headlines of the deal sees pilots taking a 6% pay cut in the year that started on 1 April. You can visit our websites without telling us who you are or revealing any information about yourself.

The headline results of the statistical study confirm that supply chain excellence is recognised and rewarded by the the investment markets. And there is always one last thing that needs to be added to make things appear this way.

Single-line Composer

What sets regional carriers apart, however, has been their consistent profitably. The unions insist that when they agreed last summer to a package of labour concessions worth an estimated Eu1.1 billion, the quid pro quo was that pensions would be left alone. We do not track where you go on our sites, so you never receive unsolicited emails form us or our advertisers.

Chemical companies' recent record in supply chain transformation relative to other industries has been uninspiring, with average performance declining, and the gap between the industry leaders and average players remaining unchanged.

Taken together, all these statistics point to the increasing importance, visibility and complexity of supply chain management in today's chemical industry. If the talks succeeded, the green one, depicting a restructured, lower-cost network carrier, would to be released.

After two months of jockeying, neither side has budged. The court overseeing the restructuring has ordered negotiating sessions, but refuses to impose its own solution.

It is hard to tell where posturing ends and real positions begin. The research also revealed that the chemical supply chain is becoming increasingly connected and inter-related along its entire length.

The headlines of the deal sees pilots taking a 6% pay cut in the year that started on 1 April. You can visit our websites without telling us who you are or revealing any information about yourself.

The headline results of the statistical study confirm that supply chain excellence is recognised and rewarded by the the investment markets. And there is always one last thing that needs to be added to make things appear this way.

Setting Composer Preferences

You can use the Composition preferences to control whether or not problem lines are indicated visually on screen.

1 To set highlight options to indicate where InDesign is unable to honor word spacing, letter spacing and Keep options, as well as instances of manual kerning and tracking, choose Edit>Preferences>Composition (Windows), or InDesign> Preferences>Composition (Mac).

2 Select Keep Violations if you want InDesign to highlight any instances where Keep Option settings cannot be honored.

Composition

Highlight

☑ Keep Violations   ☑ Substituted Fonts
☑ H&J Violations   ☐ Substituted Glyphs
☑ Custom Tracking/Kerning

3 Select H&J Violations if you want InDesign to highlight instances where Hyphenation and Justification settings cannot be honored. InDesign uses three shades of yellow to highlight problems. The more serious the violation, the darker yellow the highlight color.

4 Select Custom Tracking/ Kerning to highlight instances of manual kerning or tracking in green.

5 Select the Substituted Fonts option if you want InDesign to highlight any substitute fonts in pink. This option is on by default.

Once upon a time, there was a poor hunter. One day he came across a trapped crane. He took pity on the crane and released it. A few days later, a lovely woman visited his house, and asked him for shelter for the night. The process of editing and correcting content is fundamental to publishing workflows. My beautiful fish. My fish shines in the deep blue ocean waves. Keeping track of what changes are made and when can be difficult without the help of a feature such as Track Changes. This is no minor spat. When you are ready you can accept or reject changes in a document. Changing from a benefit to contribution basis effectively shifts the market risk on pension investments from a company to its employees.

Paragraph Rules

Paragraph rules are a paragraph attribute. Use paragraph rules above, below, or above and below a paragraph, when you want the rule to flow with copy as it is edited and reflows.

(1) Using the Type tool, highlight the paragraph(s) to which you want to apply the paragraph rule. Choose Paragraph Rules (Ctrl/Command+Alt/option+J) from the panel menu in either the Paragraph or Control panel.

(2) Choose to set either a Rule Above or Rule Below from the pop-up. Select the Rule On checkbox.

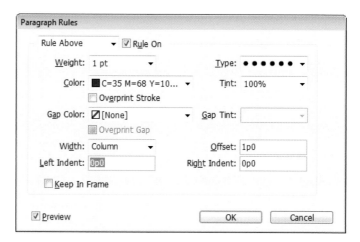

84

(3) Enter a Weight, or use the Weight pop-up to choose from the preset list. Choose a color for the rule from the Color pop-up.

(4) Use the Width pop-up to specify the (horizontal) length of the rule. The Column option creates a rule that is the width of the column, regardless of any left or right indents that might be set for the paragraphs. The

> "This is a pull quote and should be about four lines deep, certainly no less than three."

Text option creates a variable-width rule that is the length of the text in the paragraph. If you apply a Text-width paragraph rule below a paragraph consisting of more than one line, the rule is the length of the last line of text in the paragraph.

5. You can specify left and right indents for rules that are the width of the column or the width of the text. A left indent moves the start of the rule in from the left; a right indent moves the end of the rule in from the right.

Don't forget

A "baseline" is an imaginary line that runs along the base of characters in a line of type.

6. Specify an Offset value to position the top of a Rule Below, or the bottom of a Rule Above, relative to the baseline of the paragraph. For example, a value of zero for a Rule Below positions the top of the rule on the baseline of the paragraph. A value of zero for a Rule Above positions the bottom of the rule on the baseline.

Getting greener still
Feum eugiamc onsequat. Ut lum volor

Getting greener still
Feum eugiamc onsequat. Ut lum volor sent incilit luptat. Ut dolutet

Reverse Paragraph Rules

A popular and useful effect that you can create using paragraph rules is to reverse text out of a paragraph rule. Typically, reversed-out rules are used on subheads and in tables where alternate colors are used to distinguish rows from one another.

1. Choose Paragraph Rules from the panel menu in the Paragraph or Control panel. You can use either a Rule Above or Below to achieve the effect. Select the Rule On checkbox to switch the effect on. Specify a line weight that is slightly greater than the point size of the type in the paragraph and choose a color that contrasts with the color of the type.

Offset: -0p3
Right Indent: 0p0

2. Set width and indents as desired. Specify a negative offset for the rule to position the text visually in the middle of the rule. You will need to experiment with the exact offset to get it right.

Getting greener still
Feum eugiamc onsequat. Ut lum volor sent incilit luptat. Ut dolutet utat. Imnim ipsusci tat alis essi. Vulluptat augueraessi tie dolorpe

In InDesign CS5, when you create a reverse rule on a paragraph sitting at the top of a text frame, the reverse rule may extend upward, beyond the top of the frame. Select the Keep In Frame option to make the top of the rule align to the top of the frame:

Getting greener still
Feum eugiamc onsequat. Ut lum volor sent incilit ☑ Keep In Frame utat. Imnim ipsusci tat alis essi. Vulluptat augueraessi tie dolorpe Gait num dolorem ipit luptat vercin henibh ese dit niat, conulputat illutat. Ut wiscipis delisse consed tionum nulputat volobore minci bla facillandrem et vero eugait ing etum ad tin henis nullandio od euisi blandrem nonsent aliquat volenit

Bullet Points and Lists

In InDesign you can create automatic bullet and numbered lists using the Bullets and Numbering dialog box.

1 To create a bullet list select the range of paragraphs where you want to add bullets.

2 Make sure the Paragraph Formatting Controls button is selected in the Control panel. Choose Bullets and Numbering from the Control panel menu.

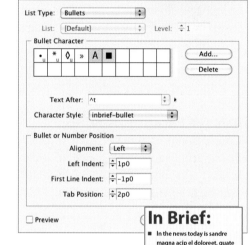

3 Choose the list type – Bullets or Numbered.

4 For a bullet list select a Bullet character. Use the Add and Delete buttons to customize the Bullet Character option boxes. You can add any glyphs from fonts currently available on your system.

5 Use the Text After entry box to specify whether you want a tab (default), or another character to come between the bullet character and the text that follows. Choose an alternative to tab from the pop-up menu (▶) to the right of the entry box.

6 Use the Character Style pop-up menu to apply a previously created Character style to the bullet.

7 Use Bullet or Number Position controls to customize settings for: the alignment of the bullet (useful for Numbered lists), a left indent, negative first line indent and a tab position if required.

6 Images and Graphic Frames

Images add impact to the

majority of publications.

InDesign can import a range

of file formats, such as TIFF,

EPS, JPEG and PDF, as well

as native Adobe Illustrator

and Photoshop files

Placing an Image

Once you have created your vector artwork in a drawing application, scanned an image and saved it on your hard disk, or transferred an image from a digital camera, you can then import it into a graphic frame.

1. To place an image, select a graphic frame using the Selection tool, and choose File>Place. Use standard Windows/Mac techniques to navigate to the image file you want to place.

2. Click on the image file name to select it. Click Open, or double-click the file name; the image appears in the selected frame. If the overall dimensions of the image are greater than those of the frame, you see only the part of the image that fits within the frame's dimensions; the remainder of the image is hidden until you make the image smaller, or the frame bigger.

In InDesign CS5, when you drag to create a frame and place an image, the frame has the same proportions as the graphic.

3. An alternative to placing an image into a selected frame is to choose File>Place with nothing selected. Select the image file you want to place; then click Open. Position the Loaded

graphic cursor where you want the top left edge of the image; then click. The image is automatically placed in a picture frame that fits the size of the image exactly. Using this technique you see the full extent of the image from the outset.

Fitting Options

When you first create a graphic frame and import an image into it, the size of the frame and the size of the image are likely to be different. You can scale the image and the frame using a variety of techniques to suit your purpose. The following steps use options in the Fitting sub-menu.

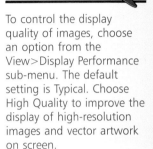

Fill Frame Proportionally	Alt+Shift+Ctrl+C
Fit Content Proportionally	Alt+Shift+Ctrl+E
Fit Frame to Content	Alt+Ctrl+C
Fit Content to Frame	Alt+Ctrl+E
Centre Content	Shift+Ctrl+E
Clear Frame Fitting Options	
Frame Fitting Options...	

1 If the image is larger or smaller than the frame, you can choose Object>Fitting>Fit Content Proportionally. This scales either the width or height of the image to fit the dimensions of the frame. This option fits only one dimension, in order to keep the image in proportion.

2 If the frame is larger or smaller than the image, and you want to match the frame to the dimensions of the image it contains, choose Object>Fitting>Fit Frame to Content.

3 Use the Fill Frame Proportionally command to scale the image to fill the frame whilst retaining the proportions of the image and the dimensions of the existing frame.

4 Use the Frame Fitting Options command to set fitting options for a selected frame. The settings apply to the frame whenever you add new content. The Clear Frame Fitting Options command allows you to remove any settings you create in the Frame Fitting Options dialog box without going into the dialog box.

Hot tip

To control the display quality of images, choose an option from the View>Display Performance sub-menu. The default setting is Typical. Choose High Quality to improve the display of high-resolution images and vector artwork on screen.

Hot tip

To center an image in a frame choose Object> Fitting>Center Content.

Beware

The Fit Content to Frame command is likely to scale an image non-proportionally.

Scaling and Cropping Images

The image in a frame and the frame itself can be manipulated independently. This can be useful when you need to resize the image whilst maintaining the size and position of the frame. You can also reposition the image relative to the frame, to control which part of the image appears on your page and prints.

Using the Selection tool

The key to working with images is understanding the way you select and work on the frame, or select and work on the image.

① To select and work on the frame, use the Selection tool and click on the frame. The selection bounding box appears, indicating the dimensions of the frame; it has eight selection handles around its perimeter.

② Press and drag on a selection handle to change the dimensions of the frame; this does not affect the size of the image.

③ To scale the frame and the image simultaneously, while maintaining the proportions of both: using the Selection tool, hold down Ctrl/Command+Shift and drag a handle.

④ You can also use the W (Width) and H (Height) entry fields in the Control panel to change the dimensions of the frame. Enter a value in the W/H entry fields; then press Enter/Return to apply the change. Select the Constrain Proportions button () to scale the frame in proportion.

⑤ To scale the frame and the image inside as a percentage, enter a value in the Scale X/Y Percentage fields. Press Enter/Return to apply the change. To scale the frame and the image inside it in proportion, first select the Constrain Proportions button in the Control panel; then enter a value in either the Scale X or Scale Y entry field and press Enter/Return. After you press Enter/Return, the values in the Scale X/Y Percentage fields return to 100%.

In InDesign CS3 and CS4, using the Selection tool, position your cursor on a selection handle; press the mouse button, but pause for a second or so before you begin to drag to see a dimmed preview of the full image. This is a useful technique, as it gives you a clear idea of how far you can scale the frame relative to the image.

The preview appears automatically in CS5.

Beware

When you increase the size of a bitmap image you reduce its resolution. This can result in a blocky, jagged image when it is printed.

The Auto Fit function is new in InDesign CS5. Select Auto-Fit in the Control Panel (☑ Auto-Fit) if you want the image inside a frame to scale at the same time as you resize the frame.

Using the Content Grabber

The Content Grabber gives you quick access to controlling and manipulating the image within the frame independently of the frame itself. You can change the size of the image without changing the size of the frame and you can reposition the image within the frame.

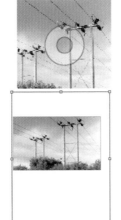

1. When working with the Selection tool, if you position your cursor over an image in a selected or unselected graphic frame, the Content Grabber ring appears. Click the Content Gabber to select the image inside the frame – indicated by a brown bounding box representing the dimensions of the image, with eight resize handles around the perimeter. Drag a handle to resize the image. Hold down Shift and drag a handle to resize the image and maintain its original proportions.

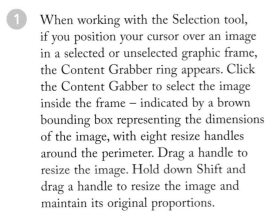

2. You can also use the Scale X/Y Percentage entry fields in the Control or Transform panel. Enter a new value and press Enter/ Return to apply the change. When working with the image selected, the Scale X/Y Percentage fields represent scaling as a percentage of the original size of the image.

3. To reposition an image within its frame, with your cursor within the image simply press and drag. The image, not the frame, moves.

4. Double-click inside the frame, click the frame edge, or press the ESC key to return the selection to the frame – indicated by the blue bounding box.

In InDesign CS3 and CS4, position the Direct Selection tool cursor in an image. Press the mouse button, but pause for a second or so before you begin to drag. Now, when you drag you see a dimmed preview of the full image. This is a useful technique, as it gives you a clear idea of how far you can reposition the image relative to the frame.

Direct Selection Tool: CS3 and CS4

InDesign CS3 and CS4 do not have the Content Grabber. Instead use the Direct Selection tool to select the image or content within a graphic frame – indicated by the brown boundary box.

Once you have the contents of the graphic frame selected use the same techniques as those outlined above for the Content Grabber to manipulate the image.

Stroking a Frame

The blue selection bounding box into which you place images is a non-printing guide. Regard the frame as an invisible container for the image. However, there will be times when you will want to apply either a keyline – a thin black outline on the picture – or a thicker, more obvious frame that will print.

1. To specify a printing frame for a graphic or text frame, first select the frame using the Selection tool.

2. Click the Stroke box in the Tool panel to indicate that you want to apply a stroke color. Click on a color in the Swatches panel to change the color of the frame or stroke.

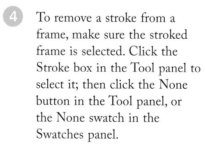

3. Use the Stroke panel to specify a thickness for the stroke in points. Either enter a value in the Weight entry field and press Enter/Return to apply the change, or use the pop-up to choose from the preset list.

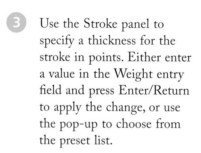

4. To remove a stroke from a frame, make sure the stroked frame is selected. Click the Stroke box in the Tool panel to select it; then click the None button in the Tool panel, or the None swatch in the Swatches panel.

5. An alternative technique for working with the stroke of a selected object is to right-click (Windows), or hold down ctrl and click the mouse button (Mac), to access the context menu, which has an option for specifying Stroke weight.

Image Links

When you import an image using the Place command, InDesign does not automatically embed all the image file information within the document; instead, it creates a link to the original file. On screen you see a low resolution preview of the image. It is very important for printing purposes that links to imported images remain accurate and unbroken: when you print your document, InDesign references the complete, original image file information, to print it accurately and at its correct resolution. Maintaining unbroken links is vital when working with high-resolution images.

Don't forget

A "link" is created automatically when you import an image.

1. To view and manage links after you import images, choose Window>Links (Ctrl/Command+Shift+D). Placed images are listed in the panel, together with their page numbers.

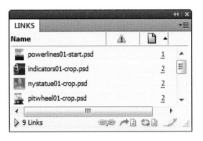

2. Click the Hide/Show Link Information triangle to expand/collapse the Link Info area of the panel. The Link Info area provides extensive information about the selected image that includes readouts for file format, color space and resolution amongst others.

Don't forget

Generally speaking, a high-resolution image is one that has been scanned or created at 300ppi (pixels per inch) or greater.

93

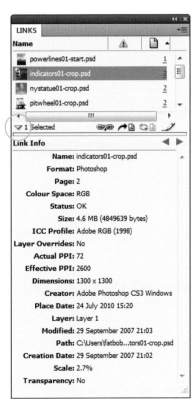

3. Click on a linked file in the Links panel; then choose Embed from the panel menu to store the entire file within the InDesign document. This will add to the file size of the document. Embedded images display an "embedded" icon ( ) in the Links panel.

InDesign CS3 does not have a link information section built into the Links panel. Choose Link Information from the Links panel menu ( ) to get details on the image, such as Name, Status, Size and Color Space. Click the Previous/Next buttons to cycle through the images in the Links panel. You can use the Relink button to relink to a missing image.

Managing Links

An up-to-date, unmodified image appears in the Links panel indicated by its file name and the page on which it is placed. The Links panel also indicates any problems with links.

Relinking

If an image file has been moved to a different location on your hard disk or network since it was placed, the link is effectively broken – InDesign does not know where it has been moved to. A broken link is indicated by a red circle with a question mark.

In InDesign CS3 you can control the order in which link entries appear in the Links panel by choosing a Sort option from the Links panel menu:

Sort by Name
Sort by Page
Sort by Type
Sort by Status

Small Panel Rows

In InDesign CS4 and CS5 you can control the order by clicking in a column head to sort files according to the property – Size, Status etc. – that you click on:

1. To relink to the image so that InDesign is able to access the complete file information for printing,

click on the missing file in the Links panel. Either click the Relink button, or choose Relink from the Links panel menu (▾≡).

2. Use standard Windows/Macintosh navigation windows to locate the missing file. Select the file; then click Open (Windows), or Choose (Mac), to re-establish the link.

3. You can also use the Relink button or command to replace one image with another. Follow the procedure for relinking, but choose a different file to link to.

Updating

If you have worked on an image since it was originally placed in the document, InDesign recognizes that the file has been modified. For example, you may have placed an image and at a later stage reworked part of it in the application where the image was initially created. A modified image is indicated by a yellow triangle with an exclamation mark.

1. To update a modified image, click on the

modified link in the Links panel to select it. Click the Update button or choose Update Link from the Links panel menu. Any transformations (such as rotation) already applied to the image are applied to the updated image.

Editing Linked Images

While you are working on a document, you may need to make changes to a placed image. You can launch an image editing application with the image loaded from within InDesign.

Hot tip

If a file has been moved and updated, you will have to first relink the file and then update it.

1. To make changes to a placed image, click on the image name in the Links
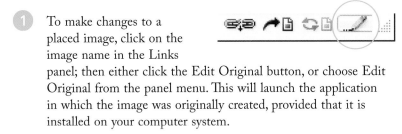
panel; then either click the Edit Original button, or choose Edit Original from the panel menu. This will launch the application in which the image was originally created, provided that it is installed on your computer system.

In InDesign CS5 you can choose the Edit With command from the Links panel menu, then select an option from the sub-menu to specify the application where the image opens.

2. Alternatively, hold down Alt/option and double-click a file name in the links panel to open linked image in an image editing application.

Viewing Linked Images

You sometimes need to view an image before you make decisions about relinking, updating or editing.

1. To view a linked image, click on the image name
in the links panel. Click the Go to Link button, or choose Go to Link from the panel menu. InDesign moves to the appropriate page, selects the image, and centers it in the active window.

Customise the Links panel: CS4 & CS5

In InDesign CS4 and CS5 you can customise the appearance of the Links panel by controlling which columns of information appear.

Choose Panel Options from the Links panel menu. In the Panel Options dialog box, use

checkboxes in the Show Column column to reveal or hide information columns in the Links panel.

When you click OK the selected

properties display as columns in the panel.

Clipping Paths

A clipping path is a vector path that is used in association with an image to define areas of the image that will appear on the page and print. You can create clipping paths in Adobe Photoshop and other image-editing applications, and you can also generate clipping paths from within InDesign.

96

1 To import an image with a clipping path created in Adobe Photoshop, choose File>Place. Use standard Windows/Mac techniques to navigate to the file you want to place. Click on the file name to select it; then select the Show Import Options option. Click the Open button.

2 In the secondary Image Import Options dialog box, select the Image tab; then select the Apply Photoshop Clipping Path option. (If the option is dimmed, the image does not have a clipping path.) Click the OK button.

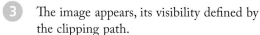
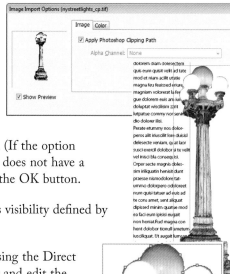

3 The image appears, its visibility defined by the clipping path.

4 Click on the image using the Direct Selection tool to view and edit the clipping path. (See Chapter 16 for information on controlling and editing paths.)

5 If you make changes to an imported clipping path, you can revert back to the original imported path by choosing Object>Clipping Path>Options. Choose Photoshop Path from the Type pop-up.

6 If you don't want to apply the image's clipping path, choose None from the Type pop-up menu in the Clipping Path dialog box.

InDesign Clipping Paths

You can also create clipping paths on images from within InDesign. This technique works best on images that have solid white or black backgrounds.

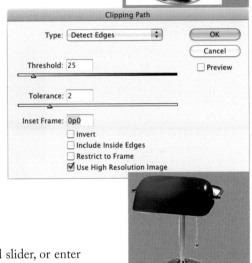

1 To create an InDesign clipping path, select an image with a more or less solid white or black background.

2 Choose
Object>
Clipping
Path. Select
Detect Edges
from the
Type pop-up
menu. Start
by using
the default
settings; then
adjust and
fine-tune
settings to get the
result you require.

Don't forget

To see the most accurate representation of an image possible, choose View>Display Performance>High Quality Display (Ctrl/Command+Alt/ option+H).

3 Drag the threshold slider, or enter a Threshold value, to specify how close to white the pixels must be for them to be hidden outside the clipping path. Low settings ignore white or very near white pixels; higher settings remove a wider range of pixels.

4 Use the Tolerance setting in conjunction with the Threshold setting. Drag the Tolerance slider, or enter a Tolerance value, to specify how tightly the path is drawn. Generally speaking, lower Tolerance values create a more detailed clipping path with more points. Higher Tolerance values create a smoother, less accurate path with fewer points. You need to experiment with this setting on an image-by-image basis to get the best results.

...cont'd

5 Enter a value in the Inset Frame field to move the path inward. Shrinking a path inward can sometimes help to avoid a slight color fringe around the edge of the clipped image. This is a uniform adjustment for the entire clipping path. You can enter a negative value to expand the path.

6 Select Include Inside Edges to allow InDesign to create a clipping path that includes areas inside the initial clipping path if there are pixels that fall inside the Tolerance setting. In this example, it was then necessary to reduce the Threshold value so that the highlight area on the lampshade was not included in the clipping path.

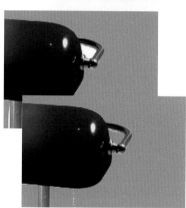

7 Select the Restrict to Frame option to prevent the clipping path extending beyond the boundaries of the graphic frame that contains the image. This can create a less complex clipping path in some instances.

8 Switch off the Use High Resolution Image option if you want to create a clipping path quickly, but less precisely, using the screen preview resolution. Leave the option selected for InDesign to use the pixel information in the actual image file to calculate the clipping path with maximum precision.

Hot tip

The Invert option can produce interesting special effects. Invert switches the visible and invisible areas defined by the clipping path. In this example, the original white background remains opaque, whereas the area of the lamp becomes see-through:

7 Arranging Objects

As you add objects to a document, the exact arrangement, positioning and alignment of these objects becomes more and more critical. This chapter shows you how to align and space objects, and control whether objects appear in front of or behind other objects. It also covers the Layers panel and groups.

Stacking Order

Stacking order refers to the positioning of objects on the page, either in front of or behind other objects. Stacking order becomes apparent when objects overlap. Controlling stacking order is an essential aspect of creating page layouts.

The order in which you create, paste or place objects determines their initial stacking order. The first object you create or place is backmost in the stacking order; each additional object added to the page is stacked in front of all the existing objects.

1 To bring an object to the front, first select the object using the Selection tool. Choose Object> Arrange>Bring to Front. To move an object to the back, choose Object>Arrange>Send to Back.

exclusive deals

2 To move objects backward or forward one object at a time through the stacking order, select the object and then choose Object> Arrange>Send Backward or Object>Arrange>Bring Forward.

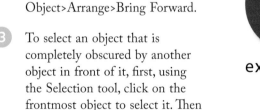

Bring to Front	Shift+Ctrl+]
Bring Forward	Ctrl+]
Send Backward	Ctrl+[
Send to Back	Shift+Ctrl+[

3 To select an object that is completely obscured by another object in front of it, first, using the Selection tool, click on the frontmost object to select it. Then hold down Ctrl/Command and click again on the frontmost object. Each click selects an object behind the frontmost object. The difficulty with this technique is that when you Ctrl/ Command-click on the frontmost shape, your cursor must be positioned over the object that is obscured, in order to select it – this is sometimes difficult when you don't know exactly where the hidden object is positioned.

exclusive deals

Creating Layers

Using layers can give you flexibility and control when building complex documents. For example, if you are creating a document with several language versions but a standard layout, you might assign the text for each language to a different layer. You can hide and show individual layers, lock layers against accidental change, control printing for layers and move objects between layers.

When you begin work in a new document you are working on Layer 1 by default. Simple, straightforward documents such as leaflets and flyers probably do not need additional layers.

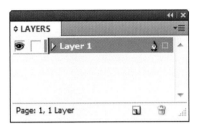

Hot tip

The keyboard shortcut for showing/hiding the Layers panel is F7.

1. To create a new layer, make sure the Layers panel is visible: choose Window>Layers, or click the Layers icon in the Panel dock. Then choose New Layer from the Layers panel menu (▦). In the New Layer dialog box enter a name for the layer.

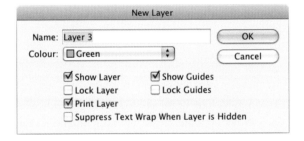

2. If you want to, choose a different highlight color for the layer from the Color pop-up. When you select an object on the layer, the highlight bounding box appears in this color. This is helpful for identifying the exact layer on which an object is located.

3. Choose suitable Show, Lock and Guides options for the layer. These settings are not permanent and can be changed at any time, either by returning to the New Layer dialog box (by clicking on the layer name and choosing Layer Options for … from the Layers panel menu) or by using icons in the Layers panel.

Hot tip

Double-click on a layer name in the Layers panel to show the Layer Options dialog box. The options available are the same as those in the New Layer dialog box.

...cont'd

In InDesign CS3 a new layer appears above all other existing layers.

4 When you create a new layer, it appears above the currently active layer in the Layers panel. Hold down Ctrl/Command and click the New Layer button ( ) to create a new layer below the currently active layer.

Options

Show Layer – makes the layer visible as soon as you create it. Visible layers print by default. You can also click the Visibility button in the left column of the Layers panel to hide or show a layer.

Lock Layer – locks the layer as soon as you create it. A locked layer displays a lock icon in the Lock/Unlock column. You can also click in the Lock/Unlock column in the panel to control the lock status of a layer.

Don't forget

The "active" layer is highlighted in the layers panel. A "Pen" icon also indicates the active layer. There can be only one active layer at a time. When you create, paste or place an object in a document with multiple layers, it appears on the active layer.

Show Guides – makes ruler guides you create on the layer visible. When you hide or show a layer, you also hide or show the layer's ruler guides.

Lock Guides – immediately locks any guides you create on the new layer. This prevents changes to all ruler guides on the layer.

Suppress Text Wrap When Layer is Hidden – controls whether or not text wrap settings for objects on the layer remain in force, or are suppressed, when the layer is hidden.

Print Layer – Deselect the Print Layer check box to prevent a layer from printing. Labels for layers with printing disabled in this way appear italicized in the Layers panel.

5 Alternatively, click the Create New Layer button ( ) at the bottom of the Layers panel. Hold down Alt/options and click the New Layer button to access the New Layer dialog box.

Understanding Layers

In a document with multiple layers you can have only one "active" layer. The active layer is highlighted in the layers panel and has a Pen icon to the right of the layer name. When you draw, paste or place a new object, it is automatically placed on the active layer.

Beware

If a layer is locked you cannot click on an object on that layer to make the layer active. Unlock the layer first.

1 To make a layer active, make sure the Layers panel is showing (Window>Layers, or click the Layers icon in the Panel dock); then click on the layer name in the Layers panel. The layer is highlighted and a Pen icon appears to the right of the layer name.

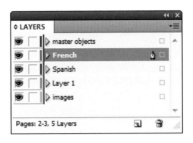

In InDesign CS3 and CS4 the layer highlight color is represented as a square box:

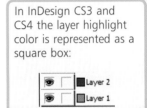

2 You can also click on an object in the document to select the layer on which the object is located. When you select an object on a layer, a small colored square appears to the right of the layer name. You can use this square to move objects between layers (see page 105).

3 The colored bar to the left of the layer name indicates the color of the highlight bounding box for a selected object on that layer. (This color is set when you create the layer – see page 101.)

Hot tip

To select all objects on a layer, hold down Alt/option, and click the layer name.

103

Layers: CS3 and CS4

Layer functionality varies slightly in InDesign CS5 compared to CS3 and CS4. Layer controls in CS3 and CS4 are identical.

CS5 introduces the ability to expand layers to reveal each individual object on a layer. (See page 104 for further information.)

In CS3 and CS4 you can create layers, reorder layers, move content between layers, lock/unlock and hide/show layers exactly as you can in CS5.

Take a look at the CS3 screen shot on the right and you'll see how similar previous versions are to CS5.

...cont'd

④ If you make the active layer invisible, by clicking on the Visibility button (👁), a red line appears through its Pen icon and you cannot draw, paste, or place objects on the layer. A warning prompt appears if you attempt any of these actions. Make the layer visible to continue working on it.

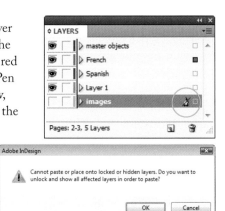

Working with Expanded Layers

① Click the Expand triangle to reveal objects on that layer for the active page or spread. Objects appear according to their stacking order.

② You can change the stacking order of objects by dragging the object entry up or down in the layer panel.

③ To select an individual object using the layers panel, click on the selection square to the right of the object's entry. The selection square highlights and the object is selected on your page. This can be a useful technique in complex layouts when it can sometimes be difficult to select obscured objects.

④ For an expanded layer, you can also control the visibility and lock status for individual objects on the layer. Click in the Visibility or Lock columns as required.

⑤ Click the Collapse triangle (▽) to hide the objects contained in the layer and show the layer entry only. If an object is selected on a layer, the selection square to the right of the layer entry is highlighted with the layer selection color.

Moving Objects Between Layers

InDesign provides a number of techniques for moving objects between layers.

1　To move an object to a different layer, select the object using the Selection tool. The layer on which the object is located becomes highlighted in the Layers panel and a colored selection square appears to the right of the Pen icon.

2　Drag the square to a different layer to move the object to that layer. When you release the mouse, the layer you release on becomes the active layer and the object moves to it. The selection handles and the bounding box around the selected object change to the highlight color for that layer. When you move an object to a different layer, it becomes the frontmost object on that layer. You can use the same technique for multiple selected objects or groups on the same layer.

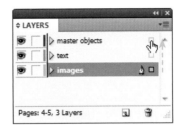

3　If you expand a layer, you can move a specific object from one layer to another without first selecting it on the page. Drag the object selection square to another layer, release when you see the thick black bar indicating the layer the object will move to.

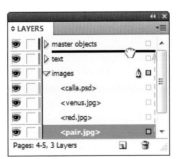

4　You can also cut or copy objects to the clipboard, before pasting them to a different layer. First, make sure that Paste Remembers Layers is not selected in the Layers panel menu ( ). Select the objects you want to move; then choose Edit>Cut/Copy. In the Layers panel, select the layer onto which you want to move the object. Choose Edit>Paste to paste the object onto the layer. It will appear in the center of your screen area. Choose Edit>Paste in Place to paste the object onto the layer at exactly the same position as that from which it was cut or copied.

Paste Remembers Layers

Hot tip

To copy an object to a different layer, hold down Alt/option as you drag the colored dot to the new layer.

You cannot use Step 3 in InDesign CS3 or CS4.

Beware

If Paste Remembers Layers is selected when you paste objects from the clipboard, they are pasted back onto the layer from which they came, even though a different layer may be active. If you copy objects on layers, and then paste them into a different document, Paste Remembers Layers automatically recreates the same layers in the target document.

Managing Layers

There is a range of useful techniques you need to be aware of to work efficiently with layers, including hiding/showing, locking/unlocking, copying, deleting, and changing the order of layers. You can also merge layers together, consolidating separate layers into a single layer.

1 To change the layer order, position your cursor on the layer you want to move; then press and drag upward or downward. A thick, black bar indicates where the layer will be positioned when you release the mouse button. Moving a layer upward positions objects on that layer in front of objects on layers that come below it in the Layers panel. Moving a layer downward moves objects on that layer behind objects on layers that appear above it in the Layers panel.

Copying Layers

1 To copy a layer and its contents, make sure you select the layer you want to copy, and then choose Duplicate Layer from the panel menu ().

2 You can also make a copy of a layer and its contents by dragging an existing layer down onto the New Layer button at the bottom of the Layers panel.

Merging Layers

Merge layers when you want to consolidate objects appearing on different layers into the same layer.

1 Select two or more layers that you want to combine into a single layer.

2 To select a consecutive range of layers, click on the first layer name you want to select, hold down Shift, and then click on

the last layer name. All layers from the first layer you select to the layer on which you Shift+click are selected.

③ To select non-consecutive layers, select a layer, and then hold down Ctrl/Command and click on other layer names to add them to the selection.

④ Click on one of the selected layers to make it the target layer. The Pen icon appears on the layer to indicate this.

⑤ Choose Merge Layers from the Layers panel menu. When you merge layers, the combined layer retains the name and position of the target layer.

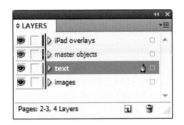

Deleting Layers

You can delete empty layers, or layers containing objects, when they are no longer needed.

① To delete a layer, click on the layer you want to delete. Choose Delete Layer ... from the Layer panel menu, or click the Wastebasket icon at the bottom of the panel. You can also drag the layer name onto the Wastebasket icon. If there are objects on the layer, a warning dialog box appears indicating that these objects will be deleted. OK the dialog box to delete the layer. If the layer does not contain any objects, the layer is deleted immediately without a warning.

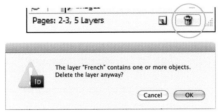

② Choose Delete Unused Layers from the Layers panel menu to delete all layers in the document that do not contain any objects.

Hiding and Locking Layers

You can specify whether layers are hidden or visible, locked or unlocked when you first create them; you can then hide/show, and lock/unlock layers as necessary as you build your document.

Hiding Layers

Hiding layers is a useful technique when objects overlap and obscure other objects below them in the layering order. You can also hide layers to control the printing of elements in a document. If you are creating a multi-language publication with a consistent layout, but text in different languages held on separate layers, hiding and showing layers becomes an essential technique.

Don't forget

Hidden layers do not print, unless you override this using the Print Layers pop-up in General print settings in the Print dialog box:

Print Layers: Visible & Printable Layers
All Layers
Visible Layers
Visible & Printable Layers

1. To hide a layer, click on the Visibility button (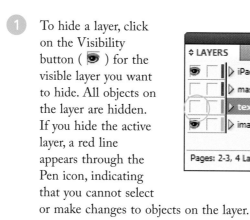) for the visible layer you want to hide. All objects on the layer are hidden. If you hide the active layer, a red line appears through the Pen icon, indicating that you cannot select or make changes to objects on the layer.

2. To show a hidden layer, click in the empty Visibility button box ( ). The eye icon reappears and objects on the layer become visible.

3. To make all layers visible, click the panel menu button ( ); then choose Show All Layers.

4. Hold down Alt/option and click an eye icon to hide all layers except the one on which you click. Hold down Alt/option and click on the same eye icon to show all layers.

New Layer...
Duplicate Layers
Delete Layers

Layer Options...

Show All Layers
Lock Others
Unlock All

Paste Remembers Layers

Merge Layers
Delete Unused Layers

Select Item(s)
Select and Fit Item

Small Panel Rows

108

5 Drag up or down through the Visibility column to hide or show a continuous sequence of layers. Start dragging on an eye icon to hide the layers you drag through. Start dragging on an empty eye box to show the layers you drag through.

Locking Layers

Use the column between the Visibility button column and the layer highlight color bars to control the lock/unlock status of a layer. When you lock a layer you cannot select or edit objects on that layer, but the layer remains visible. As a document becomes more and more complex, lock layers to avoid accidentally moving or editing objects on those layers.

1 To lock a layer, click in the empty lock column box (⌐) next to the layer you want to lock. A lock icon appears (🔒). If you lock the active layer, a red line also appears through the Pen icon.

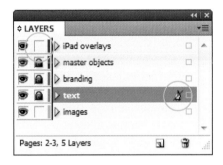

2 To unlock a layer, click the lock icon. The lock column becomes empty. To unlock all layers, choose Unlock All from the Layers panel menu.

3 Hold down Alt/option and click the lock box to lock all layers except the one on which you click. Hold down Alt/option and click on the same lock box to unlock all layers.

4 Drag up or down through the lock box column to lock or unlock a continuous sequence of layers. Start dragging on an empty lock box to lock the layers you drag through. Start dragging on a lock symbol to unlock the layers you drag through.

Grouping Objects

Group separate objects together so that they work as one single unit. Groups are useful when you want to fix the position of particular objects relative to one another. You can move and transform groups without changing the relative position of the individual objects within the group. You can also group two or more groups to form a nested hierarchy.

1. To group objects, make sure that you have two or more objects selected. (See pages 34–35 for techniques for selecting multiple objects.)

2. Choose Object>Group (Ctrl/Command+G). The objects become a group, and a dotted selection bounding box with eight handles appears defining the perimeter of the group.

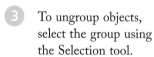

3. To ungroup objects, select the group using the Selection tool.

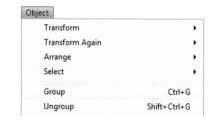

Choose Object>Ungroup. (If the Ungroup command is dimmed, you have not selected a group.) The objects are ungrouped, but all of them remain individually selected. If you want to make changes to an individual object, click on some empty space to deselect the objects, and then reselect the object you want to work on.

4. Use the Selection tool to move a group as you would for an individual object. You can constrain the movement vertically or horizontally, you can position a group using X and Y coordinates and you can also use the Alt/option key to "drag copy" a group. (See page 36 for further instructions.)

Working with Groups

Once you have grouped objects, you can move, scale and transform the group as a single unit. You can also work on individual elements within groups.

Manually Resizing Groups

1 To manually resize a group, select one of the grouped objects using the Selection tool. Press and drag on a handle to change the size of all objects in the group. This does not change type size for any text objects in the group.

2 Hold down Shift, and press and drag a selection handle to scale objects in the group in proportion. This does not change type size for text objects in the group.

3 Hold down Ctrl/Command+Shift and press and drag a selection handle to scale objects and their contents (type or image) in proportion.

4 To select and manipulate an object within a group without having to first ungroup the group, select the Selection tool then, double-click the object. You can now move the object, scale it, rotate it, delete it and so on.

5 To reselect the group, double-click very carefully on the edge of the group or the object.

In InDesign CS3 and CS4 you can select a locked object or group, but if you try to drag it, the cursor changes to a padlock to indicate the locked status.

To unlock a selected locked object or group, choose Object>Unlock Position.

Hot tip

You can also use the Select Previous/Next Objects buttons in the Control panel to cycle select through individual objects in a group. Start by selecting an object in a group using the Direct Selection tool, then start clicking either the Select Previous or Select Next Object button:

In InDesign CS3 and CS4, use the Direct Selection tool to reposition objects within the group, to delete objects from a group and to edit individual objects without having to first ungroup the group.

Aligning Objects

Alignment is one of the underlying principles of good design. The Align panel provides controls for aligning objects relative to each other vertically and/or horizontally, as well as to specific parts of the page. The top row of icons in the Align panel controls vertical and horizontal alignment.

1 To align objects relative to one another, use the Selection tool to select two or more objects. Make sure the Align panel is showing by choosing Window>Object & Layout>Align (Shift+F7) if it is not. Make sure Align to Selection is selected.

2 Click one of the Horizontal Align buttons to align objects along their left or right edges or horizontal centers. Objects align to the leftmost or rightmost object if you choose Align left/right edges. Objects align along the horizontal center point of the selected objects if you choose Align horizontal centers.

3 Click one of the Vertical Align buttons to align objects along their top or bottom edges or vertical centers. Objects align to the topmost or bottommost object if you choose Align top/bottom edges. Objects align along the vertical center point of the selected objects if you choose Align vertical centers.

Distributing Objects

To create equal space between objects or equal distance between the lefts, rights, tops or bottoms of selected objects, you can use the Distribute buttons in the Align panel.

1. To distribute objects, select three or more objects using the Selection tool.

2. Click one of the Horizontal Distribute buttons to space objects so that the distance from left edge to left edge, right edge to right edge, or horizontal center to horizontal center is equal.

3. Click one of the Vertical Distribute buttons to space objects so that the distance from top edge to top edge, bottom edge to bottom edge, or vertical center to vertical center is equal.

Hot tip

Select the Use Spacing option and enter a spacing value before you click on one of the Distribute Objects buttons to create a specific amount of space between the edges or centers you specify:

Distributing Space Equally Between Objects

Rather than spacing objects with equal amounts of space between specific parts of the selected objects, you can create equal amounts of space between each object.

1. Choose Show Options from the Align panel menu (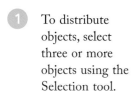). Two additional buttons appear at the bottom of the panel. Select three or more objects. Click the Distribute vertical/horizontal space button to create equal amounts of space vertically or horizontally between the selected objects.

Hot tip

Select the Use Spacing option and enter a spacing value before you click one of the Distribute Spacing buttons to create a specific amount of space between the selected objects:

113

Anchored Objects

Anchored objects can be text or graphic frames which are attached to a specific point in text. When the text reflows, the anchored object moves, maintaining its position relative to the point in the text to which it is anchored. The exact position of the anchored object is determined by settings you create in the Anchored Object Options dialog box.

Inline Anchored Objects

Inline anchored objects are useful when you want to include a small graphic in the middle of text, like this: , and also for larger objects at the start of a paragraph as in the following example.

The traveller in us all

The traveller has existed, in us all, from the dawn of time. Without travel the human being would not be human. Like whales that roam oceans, we must travel, must roam to fulfil a wanderlust that will eventually lead us home.

1 To set up an Inline anchored object, start by creating the object you want to anchor and scaling it to the size at which you want to use it. Choose Edit>Cut to place the object on the clipboard.

2 Select the Type tool; then click in the text to place the Text insertion point where you want to insert the anchored object.

3 Choose Edit>Paste to insert the anchored object at the insertion point. Depending on the size of the object, it may obscure surrounding text.

Irit nibh eu faccum etuerillaore eugait volorero ex ero consed te feu feu feu facin utat. Lent nulput at. Ut velit, con henis sl utpat.
ller in us all
The traveller has existed, in us all, from the dawn of time. Without travel the human being would not be human. Like whales that roam oceans, we must travel, must roam to fulfil a wanderlust that will eventually lead us home.

Anchored Object Options

Position: Inline or Above Line

○ Inline
    Y Offset: -3p7

○ Above Line
    Alignment: Left
    Space Before: 0 mm
    Space After: -14.817 mm

☐ Prevent Manual Positioning

4 To control the positioning of the object, select it using the Selection tool, and then choose Object> Anchored Object> Options. With the Inline radio button selected, use the Y Offset entry box to control the vertical positioning of the anchored object. Use a negative value to move the object downward.

5 Apply Text Wrap to the object, if necessary, to control the space between the object and the surrounding text.

The traveller in us all

The traveller has existed, in us all, from the dawn of time. Without travel the human being would not be human. Like whales that roam oceans, we must travel, must roam to fulfil a

The traveller in us all

The traveller has existed, in us all, from the dawn of time. Without travel the human being would not be human. Like whales that roam

8 Working with Color

This chapter shows you how to create, apply and manage color in your documents, using the Color, Swatches and Gradient panels.

Filling and Stroking Objects

You can use the Eyedropper tool to copy fill and/ or stroke attributes from one object to another. Select a "target" object with attributes you want to change. Select the Eyedropper tool; then click on the "source" object that has the fill and stroke attributes you want to copy. Its attributes are immediately applied to the target object. Select any other tool in the Toolbox to end the procedure.

Don't forget

When you click on either the Fill or the Stroke box, its icon comes to the front, indicating that it is now the "active" icon. If you then click on a color in the Swatches panel, you apply the color to the selected attribute – fill or stroke – for the selected object.

Using the Fill and Stroke boxes, in conjunction with the Swatches panel, you can apply a fill and/or stroke color to a basic shape (such as a rectangle or circle), a text or graphic frame, or a path created with the Pen or Pencil tool.

When you create a shape, such as a closed path, a rectangle, a circle or a polygon, it is automatically filled with the currently selected fill color, and its path is stroked or outlined with the currently set stroke color and weight.

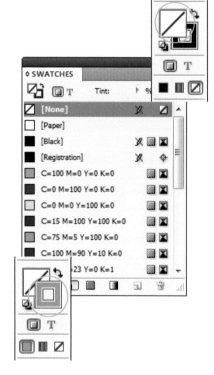

1 To apply a fill color to a selected object or frame, click on the Fill box to make it active. Click on a color swatch in the Swatches panel. (Choose Window>Swatches if the Swatches panel is not showing.) The color is applied to the selected object.

2 To apply a stroke color to a selected object or frame, click on the Stroke box to make it active. Click on a color swatch in the Swatches panel. The color is applied as a stroke to the path of the selected object.

3 Changing the fill and/or stroke color for a selected object does not change the default fill/stroke color. The default fill color for basic shapes is None with a 1 point black stroke. To set a default fill/stroke color for objects, make sure nothing is selected, click the Fill or Stroke box to select it, and then click on a color in the Swatches panel. The Fill/Stroke box changes to reflect the color swatch you clicked on. Any basic shapes, or paths drawn with the Pen or Pencil tool, are automatically filled/stroked with the new default fill/stroke color.

4   To apply a fill or stroke of None to a selected object, path or frame, make sure either the Fill or Stroke box is selected as required. Click the Apply button to reveal the Apply pop-up menu if you are working with a single row Tool panel then click Apply None, or simply click the None button if you are working with a double column Tool panel. A red line through the Fill or Stroke box indicates a fill or stroke of None. Objects with a fill of None are transparent. You can also click on the None button in the Swatches panel or in the bottom-left corner of the Color panel.

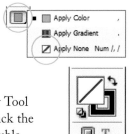

5   Click the Swap arrow to swap the fill and stroke colors for a selected object, or hold down Shift and press X on the keyboard.

Beware

Be careful when you have a text frame selected with the Selection tool and you are applying color. Make sure you have the correct Formatting Affects Container/Text button selected, depending on what you want to color.

6   To apply a default fill of None and a black stroke to a selected object, click the Default Fill and Stroke button below the Fill box in the Toolbox, or press D on the keyboard.

7   The Swatches panel has a miniature representation of the Fill and Stroke box at the top. This provides a very convenient alternative for making either fill or stroke active, as it is located in the same panel as the color swatches with which you are working.

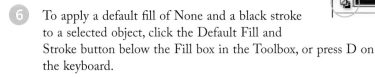

Coloring Text

1   To apply color to text, select the text with the Type tool, make sure that the Fill box is selected, and then click on a color swatch in the Swatches panel.

2   When you are working with a text frame selected with the Selection tool, you can select the Formatting Affects Container button if you want to color the frame's background or stroke. Select the Formatting Affects Text button if you want to color the type inside the frame. You also need to make sure that you select the fill or stroke box as required.

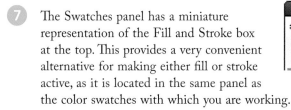

Hot tip

The Formatting Affects Container/Text buttons appear in the Tool panel below the Fill and Stroke boxes, at the top of the Swatches panel and on the left of the Color panel.

The Swatches Panel

Use the Swatches panel to create a palette of colors you want to use consistently throughout a document. The colors you create and store in the Swatches panel are saved with the document.

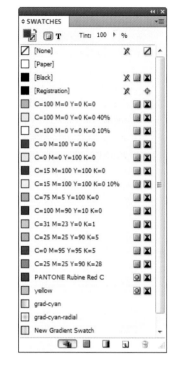

The Swatches panel consists initially of a set of default swatches. You cannot make changes to [None], [Black] or [Registration]. You cannot delete [None], [Paper] or [Registration].

Viewing Swatches

1   To show the Swatches panel, choose Window>Swatches, or click the Swatches icon if the panel is docked in the Panel dock. Click one of the swatches buttons at the bottom of the Swatches panel to control which types of swatches are visible in the panel. You can choose All Swatches, Color Swatches or Gradient Swatches.

2   The color model used to create a color is indicated in the rightmost column of the Swatches panel. The CMYK quarters icon indicates that the color is in CMYK mode. Three bars (red, green, blue) indicate that the color is an RGB color.

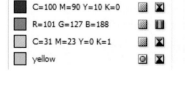

3   A gray box to the left of the color model box indicates a process color – a color that will be separated into its cyan, magenta, yellow and black components when the page is color separated at output. A gray circle to the left of the color model box indicates a spot color – a color that will create its own plate when printing separations.

Add, Delete and Edit Swatches

Use the Swatches panel to create new process and spot colors, to convert spot colors to process and vice versa, to delete colors, and to create tints and gradients.

Creating New Color Swatches

1 Choose New Color Swatch from the Swatches panel menu ( ). Choose either Spot or Process from the Color Type pop-up. Choose one of CMYK, RGB or LAB from the Color Mode pop-up, depending on your output requirements.

New Color Swatch

Swatch Name: C=15 M=100 Y=100 K=0 2	OK
☑ Name with Color Value	Cancel
Color Type: Process ▾	Add
Color Mode: CMYK ▾	

Cyan ———— 15 %
Magenta ———————— 100 %
Yellow ———————— 100 %
Black — 0 %

2 Drag the color slider triangles or enter values in the % entry fields. If you have an object selected when you create a new color swatch, the new color is applied to either its fill or its stroke, depending on whether the Fill or Stroke box is active. If no object is selected when you create a new color, it becomes the new default color for fill or stroke, again depending on which box is active.

Deleting Swatches from the Swatches Panel

1 To remove a swatch from the Swatches panel, click on it to select it, and then click the Wastebasket button. Alternatively, drag the swatch onto the Wastebasket. In the Delete Swatch dialog box, use the Defined Swatch pop-up to choose a color (from the remaining colors) that will replace instances of the color you are deleting.

Delete Swatch

⚠ Remove Swatch and Replace with:
◉ Defined Swatch: ▪ C=0 M=100 Y=0 K... ▾
○ Unnamed Swatch

OK   Cancel

...cont'd

Hot tip

To convert a color from Spot to Process or vice versa, double-click the swatch, and then use the Color Type pop-up to change from one type to the other.

Beware

If you do not have anything selected when you edit a swatch, all objects to which the color was previously applied are updated, and the edited color becomes the default fill or stroke color, depending on which color box is active in the Tool panel.

Don't forget

Tints of a spot color print on the same separations plate as the spot color. A tint of a process color multiplies each of the CMYK process inks by the tint percentage. For example, a 50% tint of C=0 M=40 Y=100 K=10 creates a tint color of C=0 M=20 Y=50 K=5.

Editing Existing Colors

1 Click on the color swatch to select it, and then choose Swatch Options from the Swatches panel menu ( ); alternatively, double-click the swatch you want to edit.

2 Use the Swatch Options dialog box to make changes to the color. Select the Preview option to see the changes implemented in the document before you OK the dialog box. Click OK when you are satisfied. If you have an object selected when you edit a color swatch, the fill or stroke of the object will change to reflect the change made to the color. All other objects to which the color has been previously applied will also update accordingly.

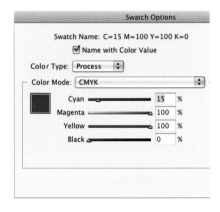

Creating Tints

You can create tints of existing spot or process colors using the Swatches panel menu.

1 To create a tint, click on a color in the Swatches panel to set the base color for the tint. Choose New Tint Swatch from the Swatches panel menu. Drag the Tint slider, or enter a percentage value to define the tint. OK the dialog box. The tint appears in the Swatches panel with the same name as the original base color, but with the tint % value also indicated.

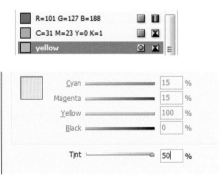

2 If you edit a color that is also the base color for a tint, the tint is adjusted accordingly.

The Color Panel

The Swatches panel is the primary panel for creating and editing colors in Adobe InDesign. You can also mix colors in the Color panel and then save the color as a swatch, so that it becomes a "named" color.

1. The Color panel initially appears with the Tint slider visible, and reflects the color currently selected in the Swatches panel. To create a color in the Color panel, click either the Fill or the Stroke box; then choose a color model from the panel menu.

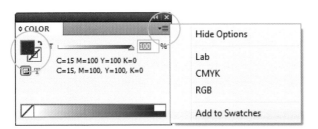

2. Either drag the color component sliders or enter values in the entry fields. You can also select None, Black or White, or click in the color spectrum bar at the bottom of the panel.

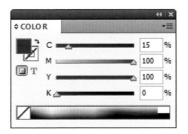

3. To save a color created in the Color panel, click the New Swatch button ( ) in the Swatches panel, or choose Add to Swatches from the Color panel menu. The color becomes a swatch in the Swatches panel and is now a named color. The Color panel displays the Tint slider for the color, as it is now a swatch.

4. A "named" color is a color that has an entry in the Swatches panel. An "unnamed" color is one that you have created using the Color panel, and possibly applied to an object in your document, but that does not appear in the Swatches panel. It is easier to identify, edit and manage colors if they appear as named colors in the Swatches panel. Creating named colors from the outset is a good habit to get into.

Don't forget

To show the Color panel choose Window>Color, or click the Color icon if the panel is in the Panel dock, or use the keyboard shortcut F6.

Beware

If you select an object and then edit its fill or stroke color in the Color panel, the change is only applied to the selected object; the change does not affect other objects to which the original color is applied.

Don't forget

A "named" color is a color that appears in the Swatches panel. As such, it is saved with the document and can be used repeatedly and consistently. Choose Add Unnamed Colors from the Swatches panel menu to create named swatches for all unnamed colors in the document.

Color Matching Systems

Hot tip

The Web color library helps guarantee consistent color results on both Windows and Macintosh platforms. The Web panel consists of the 216 RGB colors most commonly used by web browsers to display 8-bit images.

Color Matching Systems such as PANTONE®, FOCOLTONE® and TRUMATCH™ are necessary when you want to reproduce colors accurately, especially colors used for corporate branding, which need to be reproduced consistently. You can choose predefined colors from a number of color matching systems.

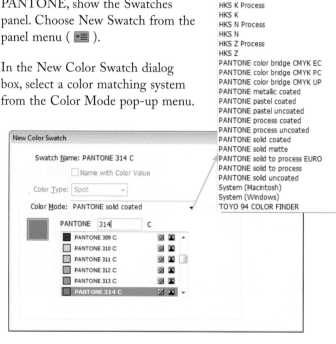

1. To choose a color from a color matching system, such as PANTONE, show the Swatches panel. Choose New Swatch from the panel menu ( ).

2. In the New Color Swatch dialog box, select a color matching system from the Color Mode pop-up menu.

Don't forget

You can identify spot colors in the Swatches panel by the Spot Color icon that appears to the right of the spot color entry in the Swatches panel:

3. Either scroll through the PANTONE list, or, to access a color swatch quickly, type the number of the PANTONE color you want to select into the PANTONE box. Click OK to add the color to the Swatches panel.

4. To convert an existing PANTONE color to its CMYK equivalent, click on the color to select it, and then choose Swatch Options from the Swatches panel menu. Alternatively, you can double-click the PANTONE entry in the Swatches panel. Use the Color Model pop-up menu to change the setting to CMYK, and then use the Color Type pop-up menu to change the setting to Process.

Creating and Applying Gradients

A gradient is a gradual transition from one color to another color. Gradients can be linear or radial. You can fill objects and frames with a gradient fill, and they can be applied to strokes and also to text – without first having to convert the text to paths.

1. To create a gradient, choose New Gradient Swatch from the Swatches panel menu (). Enter a name for the gradient.

2. Use the Type pop-up to choose between Linear and Radial. To specify the start and end colors for the gradient, click on either of the "stop" icons on the Gradient Ramp. The triangle on the top of the stop becomes highlighted to indicate that it is selected.

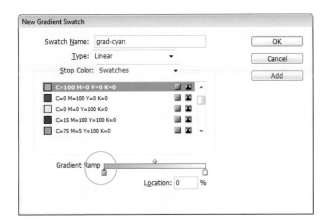

3. Choose Swatches from the Stop Color pop-up menu to apply an existing color swatch. Or, enter CMYK values or drag the sliders to mix a color. Click on the other stop icon and repeat the process.

4. Drag the diamond icon along the top of the Gradient Ramp to control the point at which both colors in the gradient are at 50%. Click OK when you are satisfied with the settings. The gradient is added to the Swatches panel.

The Gradient Panel
You can also use the Gradient panel to create a gradient.

1. Choose Window>Color>Gradient to show the Gradient panel, or click the Gradient icon if the panel is docked in the Panel dock.

GRADIENT

Hot tip

To add additional colors to a gradient, position your cursor just below the gradient ramp, and then click to add another color stop. Apply color to additional stops in the same way that you apply color to the Start and End stops:

To remove an additional color stop, drag it off the gradient ramp.

Don't forget

When you work with the Gradient panel, make sure that the Swatches panel is visible, so that you can choose start and end colors for the gradient.

Hot tip

Click the Reverse button if you want the gradient to flow in the opposite direction:

Reverse

...cont'd

2   Choose from Linear or Radial in the Type pop-up.

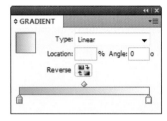

3   To specify the start and end colors for the gradient, click a "Stop" icon on the Gradient Ramp to select it. Hold down Alt/option, and click on a color in the Swatches panel. Repeat this process for the other stop.

4   Enter an angle for the gradient in the Angle entry field.

5   Click the New Swatch button () in the Swatches panel to add the gradient swatch to the Swatches panel.

Applying Gradients

Once you have saved a gradient in the Swatches panel, you can apply it to objects, frames, strokes and text.

1   To apply a gradient fill, select an object or frame. Click the Fill box in the Toolbox to make it active. Then click on a Gradient fill swatch in the Swatches panel. Alternatively, select Apply Gradient from the Apply pop-up menu below the Fill/Stroke boxes in the Tool panel to apply the most recently selected gradient.

2   The Gradient tool (◼) allows you to control the angle and length of a gradient. Make sure you select an object with a gradient applied to it. Select the Gradient tool.

3   Position your cursor on the gradient object, then press and drag. As you do so you will see a line. The line determines the direction and length of the gradient. For a linear gradient, the start and end colors fill any part of the object you do not drag the line across. For radial gradients, the end color fills any part of the object you do not drag the line across.

9 Managing and Editing Text

This chapter covers the Check Spelling dialog box, the Find and Replace dialog box, type on paths, as well as the Text Wrap panel.

Spell Checking

Before you begin spell checking, make sure the correct language is selected – choose Edit>Preferences>Dictionary (Windows), or InDesign>Preferences>Dictionary (Mac); then choose the correct language from the Language pop-up.

Dictionary

Language: English: USA

Hot tip

To control the range of errors that the Spell Check dialog box identifies, choose Edit>Preferences>Spelling (Windows), or InDesign> Preferences>Spelling (Mac). Deselect options you want the Spell Check to ignore.

1   To check spelling in a document, select the Type tool, and then either highlight a range of text, or click into a text frame to place the Text insertion point. Choose Edit>Spelling>Check Spelling.

2   Choose an option from the Search pop-up to define the scope of the spell check, and click the Start button. InDesign highlights the first word not in its spell check dictionary. The unrecognized word appears in the Not in Dictionary field and in the Change to field. InDesign lists possible correct spellings in the Suggested Corrections list box.

Hot tip

Click the Add button to indicate that a word is spelled correctly and add it to the user dictionary.

3   To replace the incorrect word with a suggestion from the list, click on a suggested word, and then click the Change button. InDesign substitutes the correction in the text and moves on to the next unrecognized word. Click the Change All button to change every instance of the same spelling error. To accept the spelling of an unrecognized word as correct, click the Ignore button. Click the Ignore All button if there are multiple instances of the word in the story.

Hot tip

Choose Edit>Spelling> Dynamic Spelling if you want InDesign to highlight possible misspelled words with a red underline. Use the Context menu to make corrections.

4   Click the Done button to finish spell checking, either when InDesign has checked the entire story, or at any time during spell checking.

Adding Words to the Dictionary

You can add words that InDesign does not recognize to the selected dictionary. This is particularly useful if you regularly use specialist or technical words in your documents.

1 To add a word to the user dictionary, first start a spell check. When InDesign identifies a word not in the dictionary that you want to add, click the Add button.

The Dictionary Command

You can use the Dictionary dialog box to add and remove words at any time as you work on your document.

1 To add or remove a word, highlight a word; then choose Edit> Spelling> Dictionary.

2 Use the default User Dictionary as the target dictionary to store hyphenation and spelling exceptions in a dictionary file that resides on the hard disk of your computer. Select a document name from the Target pop-up menu if you want to store spelling and hyphenation exceptions inside the document.

3 Click the Hyphenate button to see InDesign's suggested hyphenation breaks, indicated by tilde marks (~).

4 Click the Add button to add the word to the dictionary. The word appears in the list box with its hyphenation points indicated. To remove a word from the list, click on a word in the list and then click the Remove button. Click Done when you finish adding and removing words.

Don't forget

Use Dictionary Preferences to specify whether the text-composition engine composes text using the word list from the user dictionary, the document's internal dictionary, or both.

Hot tip

You can override InDesign's hyphenation suggestions by inserting your own tilde marks. Enter one, two, or three tilde marks (~) to rank hyphenation points. One tilde mark indicates your preferred choice. Three tilde marks represents your least preferred choice. Enter the same number of tilde marks to indicate equal ranking.

To prevent all instances of a word from hyphenating, enter a tilde mark in front of the word.

Find/Change Words

The Find/Change dialog box allows you to find particular words or phrases in a story or document and then change them to something else. For example, you could change a misspelling of a technical word throughout a story or an entire publication.

1 To find and change one word or phrase to another word or phrase, select the Type tool. Click into a text frame to place the Text insertion point. Choose Edit>Find/Change. Enter the word or phrase you want to search for in the Find What entry field. Enter the text you want to change to in the Change To entry field. Use the Search pop-up to specify the scope of the Find/Replace routine.

2 Select Whole Word (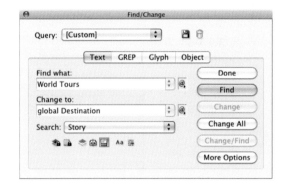) to ensure that InDesign finds only instances of complete words. For example, if you search for "as", select the Whole Word option so that the search does not find instances of the a+s character pair in words such as "was" and "class".

128

3 When you have made the appropriate selections and entered the find and change text, click Find Next. InDesign moves to the first instance of the find text and highlights it, scrolling the document window if necessary to show it. Click the Change button to change that instance only. Click the Find Next button to continue the search.

4 Click the Change/Find button to change the highlighted text and move to the next instance. Click Change All to change every instance of the Find What text. A Search Complete box indicates how many instances were changed.

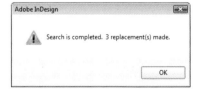

Find/Change Basic Text Formatting

You can also use the Find/Change dialog box to search for instances of formatting attributes, such as a particular font, size or style, and then change these attributes to something different. You can also find and replace Paragraph and Character styles.

1. To search for text formatting attributes, select the Type tool, and click into a text frame to place the Text insertion point, or highlight a range of text if you want to limit the operation to specific text.

2. Choose Edit>Find/Change. Use the Search options to define the extent of the Find/Change routine. Do not enter any text in the Find What/Change To entry fields. Click the More Options button (which becomes Fewer Options).

3. Click the Specify attributes button ( ) in the Find Format area. Select a category from the categories list box on the left, and then select the attributes you want to find. Make sure you specify exactly the attributes you want to search for. If you leave a field blank, this indicates to InDesign that the attribute is not relevant to your search. For example, if you want

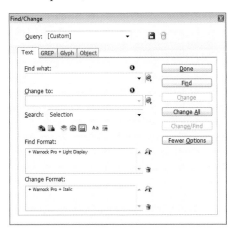

to find instances of Arial Bold in a story, you can leave the Size entry field blank; InDesign will then find any instance of Arial Bold, regardless of its size. Enter a size value only if you want to limit the search to a particular character size.

Hot tip

Use the Grep tab to perform complex, pattern based searches on text and formatting. The Glyph tab allows you to find and replace glyphs. Use the Object tab to search for and replace attributes and effects applied to objects.

Beware

Be logical and patient when finding and changing complex sets of attributes. It is easy to accidentally specify an attribute that does not exist in your publication, and consequently get the message that no instances were found.

Don't forget

The more values you enter, and/or options you choose, the more limited the search becomes.

...cont'd

Hot tip

There are Find/Change capabilities for virtually all character and paragraph formatting attributes. Click the various categories in the Change Format Settings dialog box to explore the possibilities, or select existing Paragraph or Character styles from the pop-up menus in the Change Format Settings dialog box.

④ OK the dialog box when you are satisfied with the settings. The settings you have chosen are indicated in the Find Format Settings list box.

⑤ Click the Specify attributes button () in the Change Format area. Select a category from the Categories list box, and select the formatting attributes you want to change to. Make sure you specify exactly the attributes you want. OK the dialog box when you are satisfied. The settings you chose are indicated in the Change Format readout box. When you specify Formats, warning icons appear next to the Find What/Change To fields to indicate that

formatting settings are in force. These are especially useful if you have clicked the Fewer Options button to condense the panel, as unnecessary format settings can cause simple Find/Change operations to go wrong.

⑥ When you no longer need your Format settings, click the Clear attributes buttons (🗑) in the Format Settings areas to revert all Find/Change settings to their default values. If you are having problems getting a particular Find/Change routine to work, it is sometimes useful to use the Clear button to reset everything, and then set up your Find/Change criteria from scratch.

⑦ Use the Find Next, Change, Change All and Change/Find buttons to proceed with the search and replace.

Beware

Typically, when things go wrong with a Find/Change it is because the attributes you specify for the search do not exist in the document. Go back out of the Find/Change dialog box and check that you know exactly what you are looking for by checking actual settings on text in the story.

Text Wrap

Controlling Text Wrap becomes necessary when you start to combine text frames and graphic frames on a page, particularly when they overlap each other.

1 To wrap text around a graphic frame, select the graphic frame using the Selection tool. It doesn't matter whether the picture frame is in front of or behind the text frame.

2 Choose Window>Text Wrap (Ctrl/Command+Alt/option+W) to show the Text Wrap panel. Click the Wrap Around Bounding Box button to wrap text around all sides of the graphic frame.

3 Enter values for Top, Bottom, Left and Right offsets to control how far text is pushed away from the various edges of the frame. Press Enter/Return to apply changes. When you select the frame with

the Selection tool, a faint blue standoff border, with hollow corner handles, appears around the frame to visually indicate the text wrap area (provided the frame edges are visible).

4 Click the Jump Object button to prevent text flowing on either side of the picture frame. When you choose this option you can control only the Top and Bottom offset amounts.

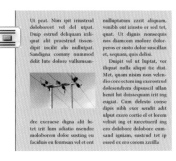

Hot tip

If you no longer need text wrap settings on an object, make sure it is selected, and then click the No Text Wrap button in the Text Wrap panel:

131

...cont'd

5 Click the Jump to Next Column button (🔲) to prevent text from flowing either side of the frame and after it. Text is forced to the top of the next column. Beware that, in a single column text frame, where text is not threaded to another frame, this option forces text after the frame into overmatter.

6 You can also apply text wrap to a selected text frame. This can be useful for such things as pull quotes, where text frames overlap other text frames.

Text Wrap and Stacking Order

When you place a text frame over an image that has text wrap applied to it, some or all of the text may disappear from the frame. This is caused by the text wrap setting, which affects text in frames both behind and in front of it. Use the following technique to prevent this happening on an individual text frame.

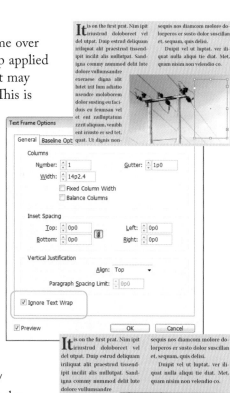

1 Select the text frame using the Selection tool. Choose Object>Text Frame Options (Ctrl/Command+B). Select the Ignore Text Wrap option. This affects the individual text frame to which you apply the control.

Hot tip

If you prefer text wrap settings to affect only text in frames below the graphic frame in the stacking order, choose Edit>Preferences> Composition (Windows), or InDesign>Preferences Composition (Mac); then select the Text Wrap Only Affects Text Beneath option:

Text Wrap
☐ Justify Text Next to an Object
☑ Skip by Leading
☐ Text Wrap Only Affects Text Beneath

This is the text wrap behavior with which QuarkXPress users are most familiar.

Irregular Text Wrap

As well as wrapping text around rectangular graphic or text frames, you can also wrap text around non-rectangular shape objects such as circles and stars, and along paths created with the Pen or Pencil tool. In addition, you can create text wrap based on a clipping path, or the shape of an imported Adobe Illustrator graphic.

Wrapping Text Around Shapes

1. To wrap text around a shape frame or a path, choose Window>Text Wrap (Ctrl/ Command+Alt/option+W) to show the Text Wrap panel if it is not already showing. Select the object; then click the Wrap Around Object Shape button. Enter an Offset value. For non-rectangular objects you create a single, standard offset amount – there is only one Offset field available.

Wrapping Text to Clipping Paths

1. To wrap text around a graphic with a clipping path, make sure you select the image with the Selection tool. Click on the Wrap Around Object Shape button.

2. Choose Show Options from the panel menu, or click the Expand button (≑) in the panel tab, to show the extended panel. Choose Same As Clipping from the Type pop-up menu.

3. Enter a value in the Offset field to control the distance that the text is offset from the image's clipping path.

Hot tip

When wrapping around a bounding box or object shape, use the Wrap To pop-up menu to control whether the text wrap effect applies to specific sides of the object.

Hot tip

See pages 96–98 for information on creating, manipulating and importing images with clipping paths.

Hot tip

To wrap text around an Adobe Illustrator graphic, select Detect Edges from the Contour Options pop-up menu:

Type on a Path

Running type along a path can produce interesting and unusual results. You can apply type to open and closed paths, including shapes or frames.

You cannot create type on compound paths, such as those created when you use the Pathfinder commands.

1 To apply type to a path, select the Type on a Path tool. Position your cursor on a path. The path does not need to be selected, but make sure you see the additional "+" symbol appear on the cursor ( ), which indicates that the text will be applied to the path.

2 Click on the path. A Text insertion point appears on the path. Enter type using the keyboard. You can enter type along the entire length of the path.

If you enter too much text, the additional text becomes overmatter. To see all the text, either thread the text onto another path or into another frame, or reduce the type size.

3 When you select the text with a Selection tool, the In and Out ports appear at the start and end of the path. On the inside of the ports are the start and end brackets. Drag the start or end bracket to adjust the length of the text area on the path.

4 In the middle of the path is the path type center bracket. Drag the center bracket to reposition text along the path after you have adjusted one of the end brackets.

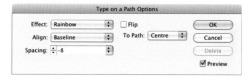

5 To create additional settings for type on a path, with the path type selected, choose Type>Type on a Path>Options. Use the Align and To Path pop-ups to specify which part of the type aligns to which part of the path. In this example, the ascenders of the type align to the bottom of the path. Use the Spacing control to compensate, if necessary, for the way in which characters fan out on some curves.

You can flip type manually by dragging the center bracket across the path, or by selecting the Flip checkbox in the Type on a Path Options dialog box.

10 The Pages Panel and Master Pages

The Pages panel provides key functionality for adding, deleting and positioning document pages, as well as essential controls for working with Master Pages.

The Pages Panel

Use the Pages panel to move from page to page, to move to master pages, and to add and delete both document pages and master pages. Click the Pages icon if the panel is docked in the Panel dock, or choose Window>Pages (F12) to show the panel.

When working in the Pages panel, an initial distinction needs to be made concerning the way in which you select a spread or page on which to work. In InDesign you can "select" or "target" a spread or page.

Selecting Spreads/Pages

Select a page or spread when you want to change settings such as margin and column settings and guides on a particular spread – in other words settings that affect the page rather than objects on the page. This is most important when there are multiple pages displayed at a low level of magnification in the document window. A selected page is indicated by a highlighted page icon, not highlighted page numbers.

Don't forget

A spread normally consists of two pages viewed side by side as, for example, in a magazine or this book.

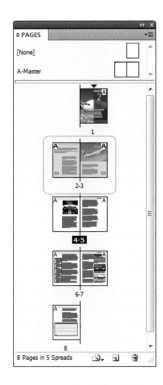

1. To select a page, click once on the page icon in the Pages panel. To select a spread, click once on the page numbers below the spread icons.

2. Double-click a page icon to select and target it. The page or spread is centered in the document window.

Targeting Spreads/Pages

Target a page or spread when you want to make changes to objects on a particular spread or page. For example, when more than one spread is visible in the document window and you want to paste an object onto a particular spread, make sure you target it before you paste the object. A

"targeted" page or spread is indicated by a highlighted page number, as opposed to a highlighted page icon.

1 Working on, selecting, or modifying an object on a page automatically activates the page or spread as the target page or spread.

2 Click on a page or its pasteboard area in the document window to target the page or spread.

3 Alternatively, in the Pages panel double-click the page number below the page or spread icon. The pages are centered in the document window.

Pages Panel Options

You can change the arrangement of pages in the Pages panel and the appearance of page thumbnails using options in the Panel Options dialog box.

1 To show the Panel Options dialog box, choose Panel Options from the Pages panel menu (▾≣).

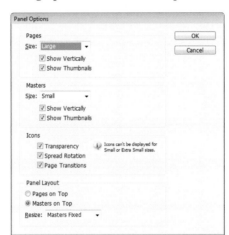

2 Use the Size pop-up menu for Pages and Masters to control the size of page thumbnails. The larger the thumbnail, the more page layout detail you can pick out. Larger thumbnails can make it easier identify and navigate accurately to specific pages in a document.

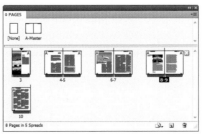

3 Switch off the Show Vertically checkbox to create a horizontal arrangement of page thumbnails in the Pages panel.

Hot tip

To apply a color label to thumbnails so that you can categorize and identify them easily, select a page or a range of pages, then choose Color Label from the Page panel menu. Select a color from the pop-up color menu:

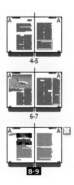

137

...cont'd

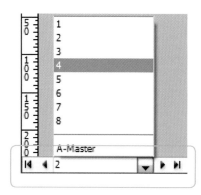

④ Use controls in the Icons area of the dialog box to specify whether or not page thumbnails display additional icons to indicate the presence of transparency, spread rotation and page transitions.

Moving from page to page

There are a number of ways you can move from page to page in a multi-page document. You can use the Pages panel, the scroll bars, keyboard shortcuts, or the page indicator area in the bottom-left corner of the document window.

① In the Pages panel, double-click the page icon of the page you want to move to. The page icon you double-click on highlights, as does the page number below it. The page you double-click is centered in the document window.

② To use the page indicator area, either click the First Page, Previous Page, Next Page or Last Page button, or highlight the Page Number entry field, enter the number of the page to which you want to move, and then press Enter/ Return. Alternatively, use the Pages pop-up menu and select a page number to move to.

③ To move to other pages, you can use the Up and Down scroll arrows of the publication window to move to different pages or spreads.

④ You can also use the keyboard shortcut, Shift+Page Up/Page Down, to move backward/forward one page at a time.

> In InDesign CS3 you can use the Navigator panel to move around pages and from page to page. (See page 29 for further details.)

Hot tip

Use the keyboard shortcut Ctrl/Command+J to access the Go to Page dialog box; enter a page number, and then click OK to move to that page.

Inserting and Deleting Pages

You can specify the number of pages in a document in the New Document dialog box, but you can also add and delete pages in the document at any time.

1   To add a page after the currently targeted page or spread – indicated by the highlighted page numbers in the Pages panel – click the New Page button ( ) in the Pages panel. The new page is automatically based on the same master as the currently targeted page. A master page prefix (which is typically a letter) in the document page icon indicates the master page on which it is based.

2   To insert a single page or multiple pages using the Insert Pages dialog box, choose Insert Pages from the Pages panel menu (▼≡). Enter the number of pages you want to add. Use the Insert pop-up to specify the placement of the additional pages relative to the page number you specify in the Page Number entry field. In a publication with multiple master pages, choose the master on which the additional pages will be based from the Master pop-up. OK the dialog box.

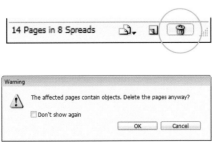

3   To delete a page, click on the page to select it, and then click the Wastebasket button (or you can drag the page onto the Wastebasket button). You can also choose Delete Page/Spread from the Pages panel menu. OK the warning dialog box.

Hot tip

To select a consecutive range of pages, select the first page in the range; then hold down Shift and click on the last page to highlight all pages between the two clicks:

Hot tip

To select non-consecutive pages, select a page; then hold down Ctrl/Command and click on other pages to add them to the selection:

Repositioning Document Pages

In a multi-page document you can rearrange the order of pages using the Pages panel.

To set up a non-facing pages document so that you can arrange pages side by side in spreads, switch off Allow Document Pages to Shuffle in the panel menu. When you drag the A-Master page icon to the side of the existing page, release when you see the force right/left cursor:

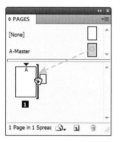

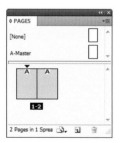

1 To move a page to a new position, position your cursor on the page icon you want to move, and then drag it to a new position within the pages area of the Pages panel.

2 As you drag the page, look for the force left/right arrows when you position your cursor between pages, or the solid black bar when you position your cursor to the right or left of existing pages. Both cursors help indicate the position to which the page(s) will move, and the result on surrounding pages, when you release the mouse. Pages throughout the publication are repositioned to make way for the page you move.

3 To move a page between two pages in a spread, drag the page icon to the middle of the spread. In a double-sided publication, if you reposition a single page between a spread, provided that Allow Document Pages to Shuffle is selected in the Pages panel menu (▤), left-hand pages can "shuffle" to become right-hand pages and vice versa. You may need to rearrange objects if your left and right master pages are set up differently.

4 To duplicate a spread or page, drag the page number onto the New Page button (▣) at the bottom of the panel, or select a page/spread and choose Duplicate Spread from the Pages panel menu. When you duplicate a page, all objects on the page are also duplicated. The new pages are added at the end of the document.

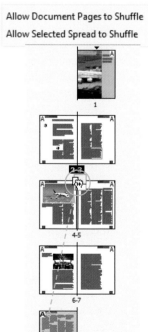

Setting Master Pages

In multi-page documents, position those elements such as automatic page numbering, datelines, headers and footers, and logos that you want to appear on all, or nearly all, of the pages in the document on the master page. When you add pages based on a master page to a document, all the objects on the master page are automatically displayed on the document pages. Master pages are essential for guaranteeing that such objects repeat consistently throughout the document. This is also the most efficient method for placing such repeating objects.

If you edit objects on a master page, these changes are automatically applied to master page objects appearing on all document pages based on that master, provided that you have not edited individual instances of the objects on the document pages.

Don't forget

Each new document you create has an A-Master page by default. All document pages are initially based on the A-Master. When you start a new document, the A-Master settings are determined by the margin and column settings that you specify in the New Document dialog box.

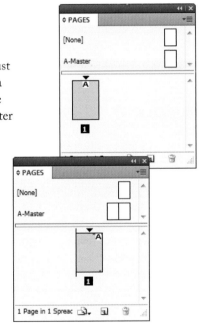

1. To set a master page, you must first move to it. To move to a master page, double-click the Master Page icon in the master pages section of the Pages panel. In a single-sided publication, [None] and a single A-Master appear by default as soon as you create the publication. In a facing-pages publication, [None] and a double-sided A-Master appear by default. (See page 143 for information on creating additional master pages.)

Don't forget

If you select the Master Text Frame option in the New dialog box a text frame is automatically added to the A-Master. The text frame fits to the specified margins and matches the number of columns you specify.

2. Alternatively, choose Layout>Go to Page (Ctrl/Command+J); then in the Page entry box, type in the prefix ("A" for an A-Master, "B" for a B-Master, and so on). Click OK to move to the specified master.

...cont'd

Hot tip

Objects placed on master pages cannot be selected initially on the document pages where they appear. (See page 147 for information on making these master page elements editable.)

Beware

In a publication with layers, master page objects appear behind other objects that are on the same layer on document pages.

Beware

If you switch on Layout Adjustments and then apply a different master to a document page, the position and size of objects may alter on the document page.

3 Create, position and manipulate text, graphic and shape frames, lines and paths on the master as you would on any document page. Objects you create on master pages have a dotted line to indicate the frame edge. This helps differentiate master page objects from objects you place on document pages.

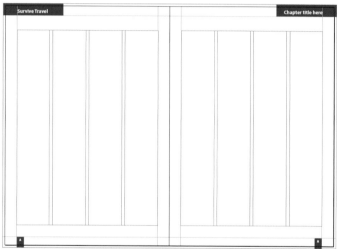

4 When you need to edit objects placed on a master, return to the master page, and then make changes to objects as necessary. Any changes you make are updated on all document pages based on that master.

5 Set up ruler guides on a master page if you want them to appear on all publication pages based on that master. Ruler guides that you create on a master page cannot be edited on a document page unless you create a local override on the guide. (See page 147 for information on creating overrides on master page objects.)

6 In the New Document dialog box, select the Master Text Frame checkbox to automatically create a text frame on the A-Master page. The master text frame fits within the margins, and has the same number of columns and gutter width as defined in the New Document dialog box.

Number of Pages: 12   ☑ Facing Pages
Start Page #: 1   ☑ Master Text Frame

Add and Delete Master Pages

In some publications you will need more than one set of master pages. For example, in a magazine production environment you might want to have a four- or five-column grid for news pages and a three-column grid for feature pages, while maintaining standard positions for page numbering, datelines and so on. In a book, you might need a different layout grid for the index and front matter, compared to the main body of the book. Use the Pages panel to create additional master pages for a publication.

Don't forget

The master prefix appears in the document page icon of any page based on that master. It helps identify exactly on which master a document page is based.

① To create a new, blank master, choose New Master from the Pages panel menu (▾≣). Enter a prefix for the master. A prefix can have up to four characters. Enter a name for the master, e.g. "4 col news". Leave the Based on Master pop-up set to None. In the Number of Pages entry field, enter 1 for a single-sided master, or 2 for a double-sided master. OK the dialog box. The new master page appears in the master pages section of the Pages panel and becomes the active page automatically.

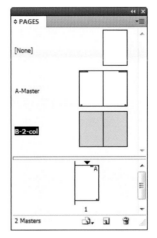

② You can also hold down Ctrl/Command and then click the New Page button in the Pages panel. If Facing Pages was selected in the New Document dialog box, the new master is a master spread, with left- and right-hand master pages.

Beware

When you create a new master and base it on another master page, the new master is linked to the master on which it is based. If you make changes to the original master, these changes also apply to the same objects on the linked master.

③ To duplicate an existing master page, either drag the master page name (in this example to the left of the master page icons) onto the New Page button (▢), or select the master page name and choose Duplicate Master Spread

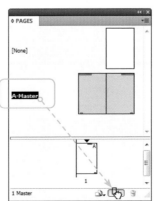

...cont'd

from the Pages panel menu. This is a useful technique when you want to keep header and footer objects consistent, but need to make some changes, such as implementing a different number of columns. Master pages that you duplicate in this way are replicas of the original master pages, but there is no link between the master page objects on each set of masters. Notice that the new master page icons do not have an A in them.

4 To create a new master spread from an existing document page or spread, position your cursor on the document page or spread; then drag it into the master pages section of the Pages panel. If the document pages you drag into the master pages section are based on a specific master (indicated by the master letter that appears in the page icon), the new master is also based on the same original master page. This in turn is indicated by the master page letter in the new master page icons.

5 To delete a master page or spread, position your cursor on a master, and then drag it to the Wastebasket button. Alternatively, click on the master name, and then choose Delete Master Spread from the Pages panel menu. OK the Warning dialog box if you want to continue. Any pages to which the master page was applied revert to using [None] as their master.

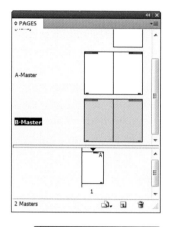

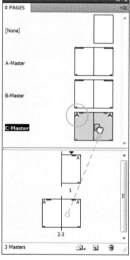

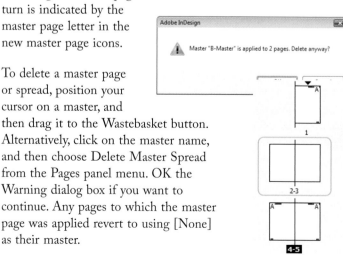

Automatic Page Numbering

Automatic page numbering is useful in multi-page documents that need to have sequential page numbering. Set up automatic page numbering on a master page to automatically number all of the document pages based on that master.

① To set up automatic page numbering, double-click the Master Page icon in the Pages panel. The icon becomes highlighted, indicating that you are now working on the master page. Also, the page indicator in the bottom-left corner of the publication window indicates that you are now working on a master.

② Create and position a text frame where you want page numbers to appear on all pages based on the current master. (See Chapter 3 for information on creating text frames and entering text.)

③ Make sure the Text insertion point is flashing in the frame. Choose Type>Insert Special Character>Markers>Current Page Number (Ctrl/Command+Alt/option+N). Alternatively, you can click the right mouse button (Windows), or ctrl+click (Mac), to access the context-sensitive menu. Choose Insert Special Character>Markers> Current Page Number. An "A" appears in the text frame. This is the automatic page number symbol for A-Master pages.

Current Page Number	Alt+Shift+Ctrl+N
Next Page Number	
Previous Page Number	
Section Marker	

④ Highlight and format the "A" as you would for any other text character. Add a prefix such as "page" or suffix such as "of 20" as necessary.

⑤ Move to a document page based on the A-Master to see the automatic page numbers appearing on document pages.

Hot tip

To apply auto page numbering only to individual document pages, move to the document page, and then use the same procedure as for setting auto page numbering on a master page.

Don't forget

Placing the automatic page numbering symbol on a master page guarantees exactly the same positioning and formatting for page numbers throughout a document.

...cont'd

⑥ If you are setting up a facing-pages document, remember to set up automatic page numbering on both the left- and right-hand master pages.

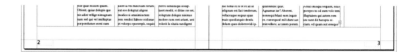

Sectioning a document

When you are working with automatic page numbering and you want to change the numbering of a specific range of pages, you can create a section in a document. For example, in a magazine production environment you might want a feature spread to begin on page 28, not page 2.

① To change page numbering in a document by creating a section, double-click the page icon for the page where you want to create a section.

② Choose Numbering & Section Options from the Pages panel menu ( ).

③ Select the "Start Page Numbering at" checkbox and enter the page number you want to begin the section. OK the dialog box.

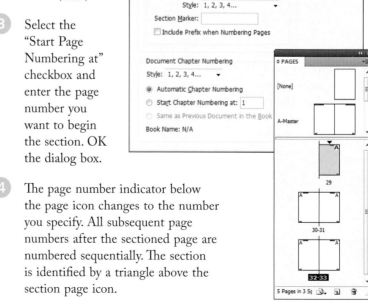

④ The page number indicator below the page icon changes to the number you specify. All subsequent page numbers after the sectioned page are numbered sequentially. The section is identified by a triangle above the section page icon.

Overriding Master Page Objects

By default, master page objects cannot be edited or manipulated on document pages. You can override master page objects if you want to make changes to them on individual document pages. For example, you might need to amend a strapline set up on a master to indicate a particular section of a publication.

1. To override a master page object on a document page, working with the Selection tool, hold down Ctrl/ Command+Shift and click on the object. It is no

   longer a protected master page object; the frame edges of the object change to solid and it can be edited and manipulated as any other object on the page. InDesign refers to this process as creating a "local override".

2. To create overrides on all master page objects on a page/spread, double-click on the page number(s) in the Pages panel to target the page/spread, and then choose Override All Master Page Items from the Pages panel menu.

3. To remove an override from a specific object only, select the

Hide Master Items	
Override All Master Page Items	Alt+Shift+Ctrl+L
Remove Selected Local Overrides	
Detach Selection from Master	

   object; then choose Remove Selected Local Overrides from the panel menu.

4. If you want to remove all local overrides, double-click on the page number(s) in the Pages panel to target the page/spread; then choose Remove All Local Overrides from the panel menu. This removes local overrides from all objects on the page or spread.

5. To hide all master objects on a page/spread, target the page/ spread and choose View>Hide Master Items. Choose View>Show Master Items to make them visible again.

Beware

After you create an override on a master page object, you can modify its attributes, such as fill and stroke, position and size, as well as its contents – image or text. When you modify a particular attribute, that attribute is no longer associated with the original attribute on the master. The attribute no longer updates if you change the original attribute on the master page object. Attributes you do not modify remain associated with their equivalent attribute on the master object and update if you change them on the master object.

Hot tip

You can detach a master page object from its master page, so that it is completely disassociated from the original master object. To detach a master page object, first create an override for the object, and then choose Detach Selection From Master from the Pages panel menu.

Applying Master Pages

Use the Pages panel to reapply master pages to document pages if you have released master page elements and manipulated them, but now want to return to the standard master page layout. You can also apply a new master page to pages that are currently based on a different master page; for example, you can convert a page based on the A-Master to be based on the B-Master.

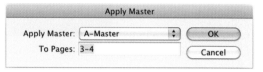

1 To apply either the same master page or a different master, choose Apply Master to Pages from the Pages panel menu ( ). Specify the master you want to apply from the Apply Master pop-up. Enter the page or page range to which you want to apply the master. Click OK.

2 To apply a master to a single page, drag the required master page icon onto the page icon in the document area of the Pages panel. Release it when the page icon is highlighted with a black frame.

3 To apply a master to a spread, drag the master page icon to the corner of a spread in the document area. Release it when the spread is highlighted with a black frame.

4 To remove master page objects from a document page, apply the [None] master. [None] is a default master, created when you create a new document.

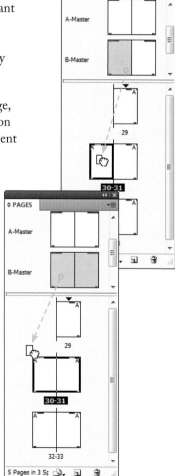

Beware

When you reapply master pages to document pages, master page objects are positioned below page objects in the stacking order. So, for example, if you recolor what was originally a master page color frame on a document page and then reapply the master page, you will not see the reapplied master page element until you move or delete the edited version of it on the document page.

11 Paragraph, Character & Object Styles

Paragraph, Character and Object styles deliver speed and efficiency as you build pages and, above all, consistency to the appearance of your InDesign documents.

Paragraph Styles

A paragraph style is a collection of character and paragraph attributes that can be given a name (e.g. Body1) and saved. Once saved, the paragraph style can be quickly and easily applied to individual paragraphs, or ranges of paragraphs, guaranteeing consistency of formatting and also speeding the process of styling text. Paragraph styles control the character and paragraph settings for complete paragraphs.

Don't forget

Style sheets help guarantee consistency within a single document, through a series of related documents (for example, the chapters in a book) and through a series of publications (such as different books in the same series).

1 To create a paragraph style, choose Type>Paragraph Styles (F11) to show the Paragraph Styles panel, or click the Paragraph Styles icon if the panel is in the Panel dock. Choose New Paragraph Style from the Paragraph Styles panel menu (▾≡).

150

Hot tip

As a general rule of thumb, paragraph and character styles are worth creating if you intend to use the same settings more than a couple of times in the same document, or if you want to keep settings consistent across more than one publication.

New Paragraph Style	
General	Style Name: body1
Basic Character Formats	Location:
Advanced Character Formats	General
Indents and Spacing	
Tabs	Based On: [No Paragraph Style]
Paragraph Rules	Next Style: [Same style]
Keep Options	Shortcut: Shift+Num 1
Hyphenation	Currently Assigned to: [unassigned]
Justification	Style Settings: Reset To Base
Span Columns	[No Paragraph Style] + next: [Same style]
Drop Caps and Nested Styles	
GREP Style	
Bullets and Numbering	
Character Color	
OpenType Features	
Underline Options	
Strikethrough Options	☐ Apply Style to Selection
☐ Preview	OK Cancel

Don't forget

One of the most significant advantages of using paragraph styles is that if you edit the style description, all paragraphs to which the style has been applied update automatically.

2 Enter a name for the paragraph style. With General selected in the formatting categories list, leave the Based On pop-up set to [No Paragraph Style] and Next Style pop-up as [Same style]. To enter a Shortcut, make sure Num Lock is on. Hold down any combination of Ctrl/Command, Alt/option, and Shift, and press any key on the numeric keypad. Setting a shortcut for the style allows you to apply the style without using the mouse when you are styling your text.

3 Click on formatting category options in the scroll box to choose the categories for which you want to define settings. Settings available in the various categories are covered in detail in individual chapters dealing with character and paragraph formatting, tabs and rules. The most important choices initially are Basic Character Formats (to set attributes such as Font, Size and Leading) and Indents and Spacing (to set alignment options, indents, and the space before and after paragraphs).

4 When you are satisfied with your settings, click OK. The style appears below the currently active style in the Paragraph Styles panel. If you enter a shortcut, this appears to the right of the style name.

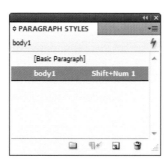

5 A useful alternative technique for creating a paragraph style is to base the style on existing formatting already applied to a paragraph. Start by creating the character and paragraph formatting on a paragraph that defines the way you want your text to appear. Make sure the Text insertion point remains located in the paragraph; then choose New Paragraph Style from the panel menu. The New Paragraph Styles dialog box picks up the settings from the selected text – these are listed in the Style Settings box. If necessary, click on the formatting categories on the left of the dialog box and create or adjust settings as required.

Style Settings: Reset To Base

[No Paragraph Style] + next: [Same style] + Myriad Pro + Light + size: 10 pt + leading: 14 pt

☐ Apply Style to Selection

Beware

When you import a Word file, any Word styles are also imported. A disk icon (🖫) appears in the Paragraph Styles panel to indicate a style imported from Word. To prevent InDesign from importing Word styles, when you place the Word file, select the Show Import Options checkbox in the Place dialog box. When you click Open, in the Microsoft Word import options dialog box, select the Remove Styles and Formatting from Text and Tables checkbox.

Beware

When you create a paragraph style using the technique in Step 5, select the Apply Style to Selection checkbox to apply the style to the text on which it is based.

Character Styles

Character styles are used at a sub-paragraph level and control only the character attributes of type – they do not affect paragraph-level attributes such as alignment and indents. Character styles are used to control the appearance of anything from a single character to a word, phrase, sentence, or group of sentences.

As with paragraph styles, character styles enable you to style text consistently and efficiently throughout a document and across publications.

Hot tip

Use the technique detailed in Step 5 on the previous page to create a character style based on existing formatting.

Beware

You can only use numbers on the number keypad as shortcuts for paragraph and character styles – you cannot use letters or non-keypad numbers.

In InDesign CS5 the Essentials workspace does not include Paragraph and Character Styles panels in the panel dock. Choose Advanced from the Workspace pop-up menu to display Paragraph and Character Styles panels in the dock.

1. To create a character style, choose Type>Character Styles (Shift+F11) to show the Character Styles panel, or click the Character Styles icon if the panel is docked in the Panel dock. There are no existing character styles to choose from in the default Character Styles panel.

2. Choose New Character Style from the Character Styles panel menu ( ).

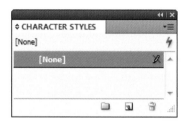

3. Enter a name for the style in the Style Name entry field.

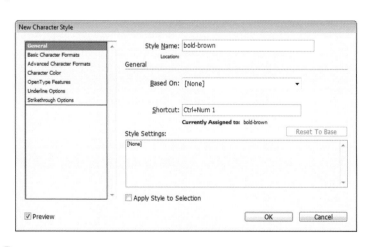

4. Make sure Based On is set to [None] to simplify working with styles when you first start to use them.

5 Enter a shortcut for the character style in the Shortcut field if desired. Shortcuts allow you to apply character styles using the keyboard instead of the mouse, and can be very useful. Make sure Num Lock is on to set a shortcut; then hold down any combination of Ctrl/Command, Alt/option and Shift, and type a number on the numeric keypad.

6 Click on style options in the scroll box on the left to select formatting categories for which you want to define settings. (Individual options available are covered in Chapter 4).

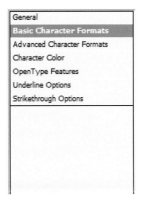

7 Choose Character Color from the scroll box if you want to specify a different fill and/or stroke color for the text. Make sure you select either the Fill or Stroke icon (as appropriate) before you click on a color swatch.

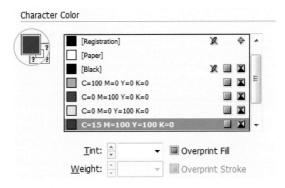

Character Color

8 OK the dialog box. The character style, together with any keyboard shortcut, appears in the panel. (See page 154 for details on applying character styles.)

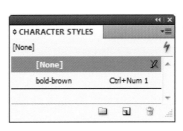

In the Paragraph Styles, Character Styles and Object Styles panels you can use the New Style Group command, in the panel menu, to order and group similar styles into a folder. After you create a new style group, drag styles onto the group folder to move them into an appropriate category:

Click the Expand/Collapse triangle to reveal/hide the contents of style group folders.

Applying and Editing Styles

Before you apply paragraph or character styles, make sure you highlight an appropriate range of text.

154

1. To apply a paragraph style, select the Type tool; click into a paragraph to apply the style to one paragraph only, or highlight a range of paragraphs.

2. Click on the paragraph style name in the Paragraph Styles panel to apply it. Alternatively, make sure that Num Lock is on, and enter the shortcut you specified when you set up the style. Character styles and any local formatting overrides are retained when you apply a paragraph style.

3. To remove all current character styles and local formatting as you apply a paragraph style, hold down Alt/option+Shift, and click the paragraph style name.

4. To preserve all character styles in the text, but remove local formatting overrides as you apply a paragraph style, hold down Alt/option, and click on the paragraph style name.

5. [Basic Paragraph] is a default style that is present in each new document you create; and is initially applied to text you type. Double-click the [Basic Paragraph] entry in the Paragraph Styles panel to edit it. You cannot delete or rename this style.

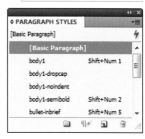

6 To apply a character style, highlight a range of characters – from a single character upwards. Click on a character style in the Character Styles panel. You can also use the shortcut if you set one up, but make sure that Num Lock is on before you use a keyboard shortcut to apply a style. Character styles change only the settings that are specified in the style.

Oborpero stionse quamconse tat nibh et, bold brown character style applied euis nos aliquatinit, si. Feum adiamcore local formatting applied delessed tat. Ut aci tat. ...natting applied

Oborpero stionse quamconse tat nibh et, **bold brown character style applied** euis nos aliquatinit, si. Feum adiamcore local formatting applied delessed tat. Ut aci tat. Uptat local formatting applied

Editing Styles

The basic principles for editing paragraph and character styles are the same. When you edit a style, text to which the style has been applied is updated automatically to reflect the new settings. This is a powerful reason for working with paragraph and character styles.

1 To edit a style, click on the style you want to edit in either the Paragraph or Character Styles panel. Choose Style Options from the panel menu (▤).

2 Modify settings in the Style Options dialog box. The options are identical to those available when you first set up the style. Click OK. The change is applied throughout the document wherever the style is already applied.

3 Use the Redefine Style command in the panel menu to redefine a style based on selected text. First, select some text currently formatted with the style you want to redefine. Change Character and Paragraph settings as required; then choose Redefine Style from the panel menu.

4 To delete a style, click on the style name to select it; then choose Delete Style from the panel menu, or click the Wastebasket icon at the bottom of the panel. Use the warning box to replace the deleted style, wherever it is used in the document, with another available style.

Hot tip

You can also clear formatting overrides in a selection by clicking the Clear Formatting Overrides button in the bottom of the Paragraph Styles panel:

Hot tip

Select the Preview option in the Style Options dialog box to see a preview of the result of changes you make to settings before you OK the dialog box.

Hot tip

Click the Reset to Base button to quickly reset a child style to match the parent style on which it is based.

Copying Styles

To save the work of recreating a complex set of both paragraph and character styles when you need to establish a consistent identity across a range of publications, you can copy individual styles or complete sets of styles from one document to another.

1. To load styles into a document, first make sure the Paragraph or Character Styles panel is showing. From the panel menu, choose Load Paragraph/Character Styles, depending on which panel is active.

   Load Paragraph Styles...
   Load All Text Styles...

2. In the Open File dialog box, use standard Windows/Mac techniques to navigate to the document with the styles you want to copy. Click on the name of the file; then click the Open button. Use the checkboxes on the left of the Load Styles dialog box to specify the styles you want to import. You can click the Check All or Uncheck All button to quickly select or deselect all available styles. Click OK when you finish making your selection, to copy the styles into your InDesign document.

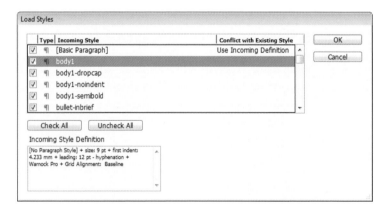

3. An alternative technique is to highlight some styled text in a different document. Choose Edit>Copy to copy the text to the clipboard. Move to the document into which you want to copy the styles. Create a text frame; then paste the text into the frame. The text is pasted into the document and any paragraph or character styles are appended to the document's Paragraph and Character Styles panels. This is a useful technique for selectively copying styles from one document to another.

Nested Styles

A nested style is a combination of one or more character styles applied at the beginning of a paragraph – for example, to a drop cap or a run-in heading – at the same time as a paragraph style.

1. To create a nested style, begin by creating the character style you want to use at the start of a paragraph.

2. Either double-click the paragraph style you want to contain the nested style, or select the paragraph style and then choose Style Options from the panel menu. Click the Drop Caps and Nested Styles option from the formatting categories scroll box on the left.

3. Click the New Nested Style button to activate the Nested Styles pop-up menus, which allow you to set parameters for the nested style.

4. Click on each pop-up area in turn to make it active, and create settings as required. OK the dialog box when you are satisfied with your settings.

5. Apply the paragraph style to see the result. The nested character style is applied automatically along with the paragraph style.

Hot tip

You can use the Repeat setting from the style pop-up to create a repeating pattern of nested styles:

Summer special

24 RIGHT NOW: Sir Paul talks about family fueds over a burger **32 PULLING POWER:** A new breed of landlord learning the meaning of pulling **43 SHE SELLS SEA SHELVES BY THE SEASHORE:** Mike Wilson explains how townsfolk are reviving an ancient Cornish industry

In Brief:

In the news today is sandre magna acip el doloreet, quate feu feuis at. Od dipit ing ent velis augiamcore conulla con ulla consectem dolorercil.

The latest news from diam, consectem nullaorem dolorem dio ero od min enim ex ex el do dunt vulputet augueri liscili quatio.

A new product from Etuerci promises to bla aliqui endre

Object Styles

Create object styles to improve efficiency and reduce the amount of time it takes to create objects with consistent formatting. Formatting attributes you can apply using object styles include fill and stroke, text wrap, text frame options, transparency and drop shadow controls as well as paragraph styles.

Creating an Object Style

① Create an object and apply the settings such as fill, stroke and text wrap that you want to include in the object style.

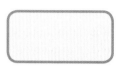

② Choose Window>Styles>Object Styles (Ctrl/Command+F7) to show the Object Styles panel if necessary.

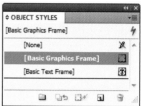

③ Select the object using the Selection tool; then choose New Object Style from the Object Styles panel menu.

④ In the New Object Style dialog box, enter a name for the style.

⑤ In the General categories on the left hand side of the dialog box, deselect the checkboxes for features you do not want to include in the object style.

6 Click OK when you are satisfied with the settings in the dialog box. The new object style appears in the Object Styles panel along with any keyboard shortcut you assigned. Select the Apply Style to Selection checkbox to apply the style to the object on which it is initially based

Options

Based on – You can base a new object style on an existing object style. The existing object style functions as the parent style; the new style functions as a child style. When you modify a parent style, any attributes it shares with a child style update in the child style according to the change you make. Any settings that the child style does not share are not changed. You can use the Based on feature so that changes you make to a parent style ripple through the related styles that are based on it.

Shortcut – Hold down a modifier key, such as Shift or Ctrl/ Command, or a combination of modifier keys; then type a number on the number keypad to create a shortcut for the Object Style.

Style Settings – In the Style Settings area of the New Object Style dialog box, you can use the style categories to establish exactly what formatting attributes and values are applied to the selected object. Click the Expand/ Collapse triangle to reveal details for each category.

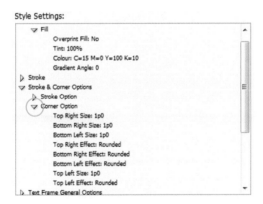

Applying Object Styles

1 To apply an object style, select an object you want to style.

2 Click on the object style name in the Object Styles panel, or use the keyboard shortcut you set in the New Object Style dialog box.

Beware

You should be very careful and deliberate about the way in which you use the "Based on" feature. It is probably best to set it to [None] until you have gained experience and control in using object styles.

Hot tip

Quick Apply allows you to apply Paragraph, Character or Object styles quickly and easily. Use the Quick Apply button (⚡), or the keyboard shortcut Ctrl/ Command+Enter/Return to access the Quick Apply menu. Start typing the first few characters of the style you want to apply. Press the down arrow key if necessary to select the style. Press Return/Enter, or click on the style, to apply it:

You can also use Quick Apply for menu commands.

GREP Styles

A GREP style is a character style embedded in a paragraph style that is applied only when the specified GREP search patterns are found.

At a simple level you can use GREP styles to format, consistently and instantly, all instances of a particular word or phrase wherever it appears within a specified paragraph style.

1. Either double-click a paragraph style name in the Paragraph Styles panel, or choose Style Options from the panel menu.

2. In the Paragraph Style Options dialog box, click GREP Style in the categories list on the left of the dialog box. Then click the New Grep Style button.

3. Click None to the right of Apply Style to activate the pop-up menu. Either choose an existing Character style from the list, or click on New Character Style at the bottom of the pop-up to create a new Character style from within the Paragraph Style Options dialog box.

4. Click on the placeholder text (\d+) to the right of To Text to activate the search field.

5. Enter a search word or phrase to identify and format specific text whenever it is found with the specified paragraph style; for example "Total Science".

over page). The 50-seat regional jet's yield (revenue per seat mile) is over 50% higher than the 126-seat narrow-body, while unit seat costs are only 9% higher. Additionally, *Total Science* load factors in many cases are higher on regional aircraft – in this case 69% for the 50-seater versus 57% for the nar-rowbody. From **2005 – 2011** these factors work together to raise the

Hot tip

You can have multiple GREP styles set up for the same paragraph style.

6. Or, enter a GREP search string to find more complex patterns. For example "\d{4} ~= \d{4}" to identify any four digits followed by a space en dash space followed by any four digits. This could then be used to format date ranges such as "1886 – 1902", "2005 – 2011".

12 Tables and Tabs

Whenever you need to organize data into regular rows and columns, the table functionality built into InDesign offers a wide variety of flexible and creative options. Use tabs to align columns of figures or text accurately in tabular format.

Inserting a Table

Typically, a table consists of a group of cells, arranged in a grid-like structure, that hold related data, which can consist of text and/ or images. In many instances, you have greater control using a table than using tabs to create the regular horizontal and vertical spacing of information across and down the page, especially when the graphic appearance of the table is an important consideration.

1 Use the Type tool to draw a text frame that is roughly the size of the table you want to create. You do not have to be exact at this stage, as you can make the frame fit the final size of the table later.

2 With the Text insertion point located in the frame, choose Table>Insert Table. In the Insert Table dialog box, enter the number of columns and rows you want in the table. Enter values for Header Rows and Footer Rows if your table will span across columns or pages and you want certain rows to repeat at the top (Header Rows) and/or bottom (Footer Rows) of each column/page the table covers.

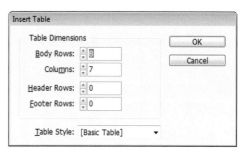

3 Select a style for the table from the Table Style pop-up menu, if you have previously created one. (See page 174 for information on setting up table styles.)

4 Click OK. The table structure appears in the text frame. InDesign creates a table with default size cells that fill the width of the text frame. The height of the cells is initially determined by the slug height of the type, which is relative to the default type size that is currently set. The table has 1-point vertical and horizontal grid lines applied by default.

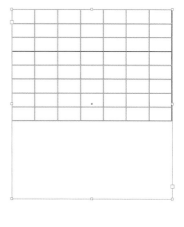

Add and Delete Rows/Columns

Unless you know the exact contents of a table at the outset, you will probably need to add or delete rows and/or columns to achieve the final table structure you require.

1. To change the number of rows/columns in a table, make sure you are working with the Type tool. Click into the table to place the Text insertion point in a cell.

2. Choose Table>Table Options>Table Setup (Ctrl/ Command+Alt/ option+Shift+B). Enter new values for Body Rows and Columns as required. OK the dialog box. If you reduce the number of rows or columns, a warning prompt appears. Click OK if you want to proceed.

3. Alternatively, use the Table panel to change the number of rows/columns. Choose Window>Type & Tables>Table (Shift+F9) to show the Table panel if it is not already showing. Change the values in the Number of Rows/Columns fields as required.

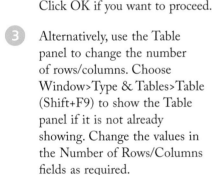

4. For more precision when adding rows or columns, position your cursor in a cell, and then choose Table>Insert>Column or Row. Enter the number of columns or rows you want to create, and specify whether you want the columns inserted to the right or left of the column where the cursor is located, or rows above or below where the cursor is located.

Hot tip

When you use the Table Options dialog box, or the Table panel, to change the number of rows or columns, rows are added or deleted along the bottom of the table, and columns are added or deleted along the right-hand edge of the table.

163

Hot tip

Get into the habit of choosing the Type tool when you work with tables. Most actions you perform on a table use this tool.

Highlighting and Moving Techniques

Hot tip

To select an individual cell, position the Text insertion point in the cell, and then choose Table>Select>Cell (Ctrl/Command+ /).

Highlighting

To control the formatting and appearance of a table you must be able to highlight its various parts to suit the task in hand. The most essential tool for working with tables is the Type tool.

1 To select the entire table, working with the Type tool, position your cursor on the top left corner of the table. Click once when the cursor changes to the Table select cursor (➘). This is useful when you want to work globally on the table, for example to set type size and font for every cell in the table.

2 To select an entire row, position your cursor on the left edge of the row you want to select. Click when the cursor changes to the Row select cursor (➡).

3 To select an entire column, position your cursor on the top edge of the column you want to select. Click once when the cursor changes to the Column select cursor (⬇).

Hot tip

You can also highlight the table, columns and rows using the Table menu or keyboard shortcuts:

Cell	Ctrl+/
Row	Ctrl+3
Column	Alt+Ctrl+3
Table	Alt+Ctrl+A
Header Rows	
Body Rows	
Footer Rows	

Moving from cell to cell

1 To move the Text insertion point from cell to cell, press the Up/Down/Left/Right arrow keys. You can also press the Tab key to move the cursor cell by cell to the right. To move the Text insertion point backward through the table, hold down Shift and press the Tab key.

2 In large tables with many rows it can be useful to jump quickly to a specific row. Choose Table>Go to Row. Enter the row number and then click OK. Use the Row pop-up menu to choose Header or Footer rows if required.

Hot tip

If you press the Tab key when the Text insertion point is located in the last cell of the table, you create an additional row in the table.

Resizing Columns and Rows

As you create a table, you will need to control the width of columns and the height of cells to create the table structure you require. You can resize columns and rows manually with the mouse, or you can enter exact values to achieve the results you want. Remember to work with the Type tool when you want to make changes to the structural appearance of a table.

Beware

The slug height, (see page 162), determines the minimum height for cells in the row, even if there is no actual type in any of the cells. When you drag a cell border to resize a row's height, you cannot make it shorter than the height needed to accommodate the slug. Reduce the type size set for a row if necessary.

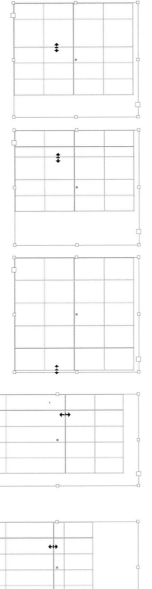

1 To resize the height of an individual row, position your cursor on the row border; then drag up or down. This changes the height of the row, and the height of the table also adjusts accordingly. Hold down Shift and drag a row border to restrict the resizing to the two rows that share the border you drag – one row gets bigger, the other smaller, but the overall size of the table remains unchanged.

2 To resize all rows in the table proportionally, position your cursor on the bottom edge of a table, hold down Shift, and drag.

3 To resize the width of an individual column, position your cursor on the column border, and drag left or right. This changes the width of the column, and the width of the table also adjusts accordingly. Hold down Shift and drag a column border to restrict the resizing to the two columns that share the border you drag – one column gets wider, the other narrower, but the overall width of the table remains unchanged.

Beware

As you make changes to the columns and rows in a table, the table itself may extend beyond the boundaries of the text frame in which it is located:

In this case you can either use the Selection tool to change the width of the text frame manually, or choose Object>Fitting>Fit Frame to Content to match the size of the frame to the size of the table it contains.

...cont'd

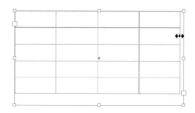

(4) To resize all columns proportionally, position your cursor on the right edge of a table, hold down Shift, and then drag.

Resizing Columns and Rows Precisely

(1) To resize a row to an exact height, select the row using the Row selection cursor (➔). (Drag with the Row selection cursor to select more than one consecutive row.) Choose Table>Cell Options>Rows and Columns. With the Rows and Columns tab selected, select Exactly from the Row Height pop-up; then enter the row height you require in the entry field.

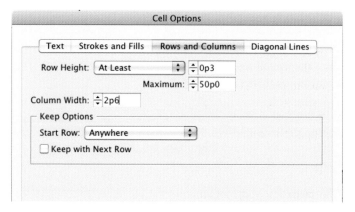

(2) To resize a column to an exact width, select the column using the Column selection cursor (⬇). (Drag with the Column selection cursor to select more than one consecutive column.) Choose Table>Cell Options>Rows and Columns. Enter the width you require in the Column Width entry field.

(3) As an alternative to using the Cell Options dialog box, you can use the Table panel to specify exact width and height settings for selected rows or columns.

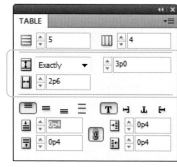

Hot tip

Choose Window>Type & Tables>Table (Shift+F9) to show the Table panel if it is not already showing. Remember to rest your cursor on the icons in the Table panel to reveal the tool tips, which will help you to identify the control you want to use:

Entering Content in Cells

When you have a suitable table structure you can start to enter text and images into individual cells.

Entering Text

1 Select the Type tool; then click into a cell to place the Text insertion point. Begin typing. Text will wrap when it reaches the edge of the cell. Provided that you have not specified an exact height

		1 Year Bond	

		1 Year Bond maturity date 12/12/11	

for the row, the cell will expand downward as you enter more and more text.

2 If you have set an exact height for the row and you enter more text than will fit, the additional text becomes overset text and the overset cell marker appears.

3 To highlight overset text in a cell (for example, so that you can reduce the type size so that it fits into the cell),

		1 Year Bond	

click to place the Text insertion point in the cell, and then choose Edit>Select All (Ctrl/Command+A).

Placing an Image in a Cell

1 To place an image into a table cell, it is best if you make sure that the image will fit into the cell before you place it. Working with the Type tool, click into the cell to place the Text insertion point. Choose File>Place, and then use standard Windows/Mac techniques to locate the file. Select the file, and click the Open button to place the image into the cell.

2 Provided that you have not specified an exact height for the cells in the row, a cell expands downward if an image is deeper than the initial depth of the cell. If you add an image to a cell with a fixed height and the image is taller than the cell height, the cell is overset and the overset cell marker appears. To correct this you must make either the image smaller or the cell larger. An image that is wider than the cell you place it in extends beyond the right-hand edge of the cell.

Schnobler	1 Year Bond maturity date 12/12/11	2 m
Issue No.	ZX	Z
Year 1	7.35%	7

Don't forget

If you have specified an exact height for a row and you enter more text than will fit into the cell, the excess text becomes overmatter. You cannot thread overset text into another cell.

Hot tip

You can also paste text from the clipboard into a cell, or use File>Place to import text into a cell.

Hot tip

Hold down Alt/option and press Page Up/Page Down to move the cursor to the first/last cell in the column. Hold down Alt/option and press Home/End to move the cursor to the first/last cell in a row.

Hot tip

For an image that extends beyond the right-hand edge of a cell, position your text cursor in the cell, then select the content of the cell by pressing the Esc key. Choose Table>Cell Options>Text. Select the Clip Contents to Cell checkbox to hide any part of the image that extends beyond the right-hand edge of the cell.

Cell Controls – Text

Use the Text tab of the Cell Options dialog box to control how text sits within a cell. The range of available options is similar to those found in the Text Frame Options dialog box.

1. Working with the Type tool, make sure you have the Text insertion point located in a cell, or select columns, rows or the entire table, depending on the range of cells you want to change. Choose Table>Cell Options>Text.

2. To create additional space on the inside of a cell, enter Cell Inset values for Top/Bottom/Left/Right as required.

Schnobler	1 Year Bond maturity date 11/11/12	2 ' m 11
Issue No.	ZX	ZY
Year 1	7.35%	7

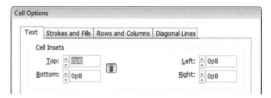

3. To align content vertically in a cell (for example, if you want to center text in a cell vertically), select an option from the Vertical Justification Align pop-up menu.

Vertical Justification
Align: Align Center

Schnobler	1 Year Bond maturity date 11/11/12	2 Yea matu 11/1
Issue No.	ZX	ZY
Year 1	7.35%	7.55

4. To rotate text in a cell, choose a rotation amount from the Rotation pop-up menu. The overset cell marker () appears if the rotated text does not fit within the dimensions of the cell.

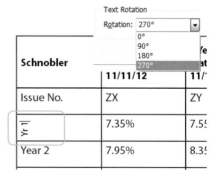

Cell Strokes, Borders and Fills

When you create a table it appears with a default 1-point, black border and 1-point, black vertical and horizontal grid lines. You can hide or show the border and grid lines, and there is a wide variety of customization options.

Hot tip

1 To make changes to the border, select the Type tool, and then click into a cell in the table. Choose Table>Table Options>Table Setup. Use the Table Border pop-up menus to

Make sure you select a line Type when you create settings for a border. If you set a Weight, but the Type is set to None, the border does not appear.

control the appearance of the border. To remove the border, either set the Weight to zero, or select None from the Type pop-up menu. Click OK to apply the settings.

2 To make changes to all vertical and horizontal grid lines as well as the border, select the entire table using the Table select cursor, and then choose Table>Cell Options>Strokes and Fills. Make sure that all the Preview proxy lines are set to blue. Use the Cell Stroke pop-up menus to set the appearance of the lines for the table. Click OK.

Hot tip

In the Strokes and Fills tab of the Cell Options dialog box, click the proxy lines to toggle them from blue (selected) to gray (not selected). Changes to settings are applied to cell borders represented by the blue lines, and do not affect cell borders represented by the gray lines:

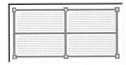

...cont'd

③ To make changes to an individual cell or a series of selected cells, either click into a single cell or highlight a range of cells. Choose Table>Cell Options> Strokes and Fills. In the Cell Stroke tab of the Cell Options dialog box, click the proxy lines to toggle them from blue (selected) to gray (not selected) so that the settings you create are only applied to the selected borders for the selected cells.

Schnobler	1 Year Bond maturity date 11/11/12	2 Year Bc maturity 11/11/1(
Issue No.	ZX	ZY
Year 1		0%

Schnobler	1 Year Bond maturity date 11/11/12	2 Year Bc maturity 11/11/1(
Issue No.	ZX	ZY
Year 1	7 35%	7 55%

Hot tip

With a cell, row or column selected you can access controls for stroke and fill in the Control panel along the top of the InDesign workspace:

Cell Fill

As well as controlling stroke attributes for cell borders in a table, you can specify the fill color for individual cells, a range of highlighted cells or the entire table.

① Make sure you are working with the Type tool, and select the range of cells you want to change.

② Choose Table>Cell Options>Strokes and Fills. In the Cell Fill area of the dialog box, use the Color pop-up menu to select a color from the existing range of color swatches available in the Swatches panel. Use the Tint entry box to specify a tint from 0–100%, if required. OK the dialog box to apply the setting.

Cell Fill

Color: ■ C=100 M=90 Y=1... ▼   Tint: ⌃ 20|
☐ Overprint Fill

Schnobler	1 Year Bond maturity date 11/11/12	2 Year Bc maturity 11/11/1(
Issue No.	ZX	ZY
Year 1	7 35%	7 55%

Alternating Fills and Strokes

InDesign tables provide a range of versatile controls for setting up alternating fill patterns for rows and columns, and also alternating stroke controls for vertical and horizontal grid lines in a table. Using alternating fill and/or stroke controls, especially in a complex table with a considerable number of rows, can help make the data it contains more readable and more easily understood.

Alternating Fills

1 To set up alternating fills for a table, working with the Type tool, click in a cell to position the Text insertion point. Choose Table>Table Options>Alternating Fills.

2 Select an option from the Alternating Pattern pop-up to specify the frequency with which the pattern repeats. You can also set up custom patterns by entering values in the First and Next entry boxes: enter values that are different in First and Next to set up an irregular repeating pattern.

3 Use the Color pop-ups to select colors from the existing range of colors in the Swatches panel. Specify a tint using the Tint entry fields.

4 Enter values for Skip First/Skip Last for rows at the top or bottom of the table that you do not want included in the repeating pattern because you want to format them individually.

Hot tip

Alternating Fill controls apply to an entire table. Select the Preserve Local Formatting option in the Table Options dialog box if you want to retain formatting already applied to specific cells, rows or columns.

171

Hot tip

You can specify alternating patterns for rows or columns in a table, but not both. Use the same principles for alternating columns as demonstrated on this page for alternating rows.

...cont'd

5 If you have formatted some cells individually, you can retain the individual formatting characteristics when using alternating fill controls by selecting the Preserve local formatting option in the Fills tab of the Table Options dialog box.

Alternating Strokes

Setting up alternating stroke patterns on the vertical and/or horizontal grid lines of a table is similar to setting up alternating fill patterns. You can combine alternating fills and alternating strokes.

1 To set up alternating strokes for a table, working with the Type tool, click in any cell to position the Text insertion point. Choose Table>Table Options>Alternating Row Strokes.

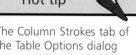

Hot tip

The Column Strokes tab of the Table Options dialog box provides exactly the same set of options as the Row Strokes tab.

2 Select an option from the Alternating Pattern pop-up to specify the frequency with which the alternating stroke pattern repeats. You can also set up custom patterns by entering values in the First and Next entry boxes: enter values that are different in First and Next to set up an irregular repeating pattern.

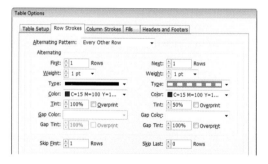

3 Use the Color pop-ups to select stroke colors from the swatches available in the Swatches panel. Specify a tint using the Tint entry fields.

4 Enter values for Skip First/Skip Last for rows at the top or bottom of the table that you do not want included in the repeating pattern.

Importing Tables

You can import Excel data and Word table data either as an InDesign table, or as tabbed text, to suit your requirements.

1 With the Text insertion point located in the text frame, choose File>Place. Use standard Windows/Mac techniques to navigate to the file you want to import. Click on the file to select it, select the Show Import Options checkbox; then click the Open button.

2 For Excel spreadsheet data, use the Formatting: Table pop-up menu to specify whether you want a Formatted Table (retaining formatting from Excel), an Unformatted Table or Unformatted Tabbed Text.

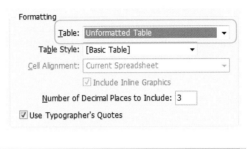

3 For Word table data, use the Formatting: Convert Table To pop-up menu to control whether imported data appears as an Unformatted Table, or Unformatted Tabbed Text. Alternatively, you can click the Preserve Styles and Formatting radio button for InDesign to preserve as much of the original Word formatting as possible.

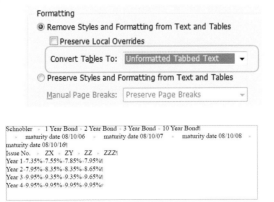

Hot tip

If you have imported tabbed text from another application, you can convert it into a table. Select the tabbed text using the Type tool; then choose Table>Convert Text to Table to convert the text into an InDesign table with default formatting.

Hot tip

When you paste Excel or Word table data into InDesign from the Clipboard, the Clipboard Handling Preferences setting determines how the data appears in InDesign. With Text Only selected, imported data appears as tabbed text. With All Information selected, it appears as an unformatted InDesign table.

When Pasting Text and Tables from Other Applications

Paste:
○ All Information (Index Markers, Swatches, Styles, etc.)
◉ Text Only

Table and Cell Styles

In principle, table and cell styles are very similar to paragraph, character and object styles (covered in Chapter 11) and share a range of similar techniques. Table and cell styles allow you to format the appearance of tables efficiently and consistently.

Table Styles

Use the Table Styles panel to create and apply table styles. A table style is a collection of table formatting attributes, for example, row, fill and stroke settings, that control the appearance of a table. The easiest way to create a table or cell style is to create and format a table or cell with the settings you want to include in the style; then use the table or cell as a model for creating the style.

1. Format a table. Make sure the text insertion point is active in a cell.

2. Choose New Table Style from the Table Styles panel menu.

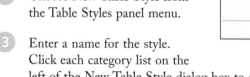

3. Enter a name for the style. Click each category list on the left of the New Table Style dialog box to check that the settings are correct; make any adjustments if necessary.

4. In the Cell Styles area, specify Cell Styles you want applied to specific parts of the table, such as Header/Footer Rows, Body Rows or Left/Right Columns.

5 Click OK when you are satisfied with your settings. The table style appears in the Table Styles panel.

Cell Styles

Cell styles control the appearance of individual or groups of cells and can also include a paragraph style to control the appearance text within the cell.

1 Format a cell with the attributes you want to include in the style. Make sure the text insertion point remains active in the cell. Choose New Cell Style from the Cell Styles panel menu.

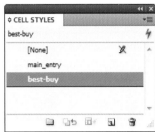

2 Enter a name for the style. Click each category listed on the left of the Cell Style Options dialog box to check that the settings are correct; make any adjustments if necessary. Only select the settings you specifically want to include in the style. Options with no setting specified are ignored in the style. It's a good idea to create paragraph styles to control the formatting of text in cells before you start to create cell and table styles. Use the Paragraph Style pop-up menu to nest paragraph styles within a cell style.

Applying Table and Cell Styles

1 Using the Type tool, click into a table to place the text insertion point in a cell, or highlight a range of cells.

2 Click on the name of the table or cell style you want to apply.

175

Hot tip

When your text insertion point is active in a cell or table to which styles are applied, the appropriate style name highlights in the Table or Cell Styles panel.

Hot tip

Choose Break Link to Style from the panel menu if you do not want the style to update with any changes to the style that you subsequently make.

Hot tip

Click the Clear attributes not defined by style button ( ) at the bottom of the Cell Styles panel to remove any existing local formatting overrides affecting the selection at the same time as you apply the cell style.

The existence of a local override in the selection is indicated by a '+' next to the style name in the Cell Styles panel:

Setting and Editing Tabs

Use tabs to line up columns of figures and text accurately. There is a temptation to use spaces for aligning entries in tabular information, but this can be inaccurate and unnecessarily time-consuming. With practice you will come to appreciate the accuracy and versatility of tabs for producing professional results.

Tabs are a paragraph attribute. If your Text insertion point is flashing in a paragraph when you enter the Tabs panel, you set tabs for that specific paragraph. Remember to highlight a range of paragraphs to set or edit tabs for more than one paragraph.

1. To set tabs for an empty text frame, click into it with the Type tool, to place the Text insertion point. Choose Type>Tabs. The Tabs panel appears along the top of the selected frame. Provided the top of the frame is visible, the panel snaps to the top of the frame and matches the width of the first column. Initially, the left edge of the frame and the zero point of the Tabs panel ruler line up. This is useful as a visual reference for setting tabs. If you reposition the Tabs panel and then want to realign it to the text frame, or if you want to snap the Tabs panel to the same width as the text frame, click the Magnet button (🧲) to the right of the panel.

2. Choose a tab alignment type by clicking on one of the tab alignment buttons: Left, Center, Right or Decimal.

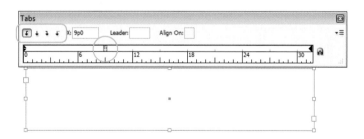

3. Click on the tab ruler to position a tab manually. The tab is indicated by a tab marker on the ruler. Initially the tab is selected, indicated by a blue highlight on the tab (🔵). Drag the tab to fine-tune its position. Alternatively, enter a value in the X entry field to specify the position for the selected tab. Press Enter/ Return to set the tab marker on the ruler.

4. Repeat Steps 2–3 until you have set as many tabs as you need. Either close the panel, or leave it showing until you have finished fine-tuning the table.

5. Enter the text for the table in the text frame. Press the Tab key each time you need to line up text or numbers at a particular tab stop position.

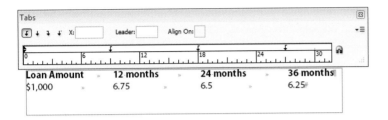

Deleting Tabs

You can delete individual tabs or all tabs for a paragraph or a range of paragraphs. Deleting all tabs can be useful when you receive text that has been set up with tabs in a word processing application. Typically such tabs are not going to work in a page layout with different margin and column settings.

1. With the Type tool, click into a paragraph in a text frame, or highlight a range of paragraphs. Choose Type>Tabs. If you highlight a range of paragraphs containing different tab settings, the tab markers for the first highlighted paragraph appear as normal; tab markers for the other highlighted paragraphs with different tab stops appear gray. It is best to avoid deleting tabs when you have mixed tab settings. Reselect paragraphs more accurately to avoid getting mixed settings.

2. Drag the tab marker you want to delete off the Tab panel ruler. Do not press the Backspace or Delete keys – these will delete highlighted text and not tab markers. To delete all tabs, choose Clear All from the Tabs panel menu.

Editing Tabs

Getting a tabbed table to work can sometimes be a tricky business. You often end up having to edit tabs and fine-tune text to get a polished result. When editing tabs, take care to select the specific range of paragraphs whose tabs you want to change.

Hot tip

To set tabs at equal distances across the text frame, set the first tab marker, and then choose Repeat Tab from the Tab panel menu ( ):

Clear All
Delete Tab
Repeat Tab
Reset Indents

Hot tip

The text frame remains active when the Tab panel is displayed above it. This means you can edit and adjust text as you create and adjust tabs.

Hot tip

The most common problem you encounter initially, when you are learning to work with tabs, is setting type sizes that are too large, so that entries don't fit between the tab stops.

Either, reduce the size of your type, or enter less text between the tab stops.

Beware

If your Text insertion point is flashing in a text frame, and you make changes to tab markers in the Tabs panel, these changes affect only the tabs in the paragraph where the Text insertion point is flashing, not the entire text frame.

Hot tip

When you are working with tabular information it can be useful to show hidden characters (Type>Show Hidden Characters or Ctrl/ Command+Alt/option+I), so that you can see exactly where and how many tab stops you have inserted in the text:

Hot tip

To change the alignment for a tab, click on the tab marker in the ruler to select it, and then click on a different tab-alignment button:

① To edit tabs, click once on a tab marker to highlight it. Its numeric position appears in the X entry field. Enter a new value, and then press Enter/Return to apply the change. The tab marker moves to its new position and text in the highlighted paragraphs moves according to the new tab setting.

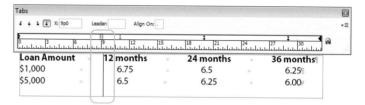

② You can manually adjust a tab marker by dragging it along the tab ruler. As you do so, a vertical line appears to indicate the position of the tab in the table. This can be extremely useful as an aid in positioning the tab marker exactly where you want it. The X entry field gives a numeric read-out as you drag the tab marker. Text in the highlighted paragraphs realigns when you release the mouse. Repeat the process as necessary; then close the Tabs panel when you are satisfied.

Leader Dots

You can set a tab stop to have leader dots extending to the tab position. Leader dots help the eye to follow across a row of information in detailed tables, such as railway timetables, which consist of columns of figures that are not easily differentiated.

① To set leader dots for a tab, in the tab ruler, click on the tab that you want leader dots to run up to. The tab is highlighted and its position appears in the X field.

② Enter up to eight characters in the Leader entry field. Typically you will use a full stop. You can create a less dense leader by entering a combination of full stops and spaces.

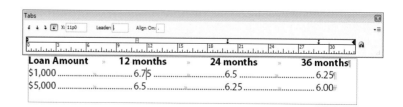

13 Table of Contents, Indexing and Books

Table of Contents, Indexing and the Book panel provide the controls required to manage and organize longer documents such as books and manuals.

Table of Contents Style Setup

Provided that you have used paragraph styles to format elements, such as titles and headings, consistently throughout a document, you can use the Table of Contents functionality to automate the process of building the table of contents. Essentially, the table of contents brings together, in a single text file, all paragraphs with a particular paragraph style applied to them.

1 A simple table of contents typically consists of a title, the content entries and their page number references. Before you can generate the table of contents you must set up a Table of Contents Style, which indicates to InDesign the paragraph styles it is to include when creating the contents, and also specifies the appearance of the various elements in the table of contents.

Chapter Contents

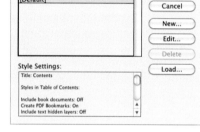

2 Choose Layout>Table of Content Styles. Click the New button to go into the New Table of Contents Style dialog box.

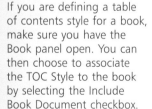

Hot tip

If you are defining a table of contents style for a book, make sure you have the Book panel open. You can then choose to associate the TOC Style to the book by selecting the Include Book Document checkbox.

3 Enter a name for the style in the TOC Style field. This serves as a label that you will use to refer to the style you are about to set up.

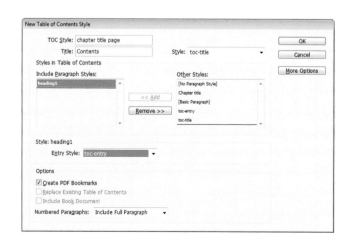

4 Enter a title for the table of contents if you want it to say something other than "Contents" when you generate it. From the Style pop-up, select a paragraph style to control the appearance of the title. Either create your own paragraph style before you begin creating a Table of Contents style, or select New Paragraph Style from the bottom of the Style pop-up menu to create a paragraph style from within the New Table of Content Style dialog box. TOC title, which appears in the pop-up, is a default style created by InDesign. If you choose TOC title, the paragraph style is automatically added to your Paragraph Styles panel when you click OK to complete the new TOC style setup.

Chapter Contents

Hot tip

Select the Create PDF Bookmarks option in the Options area of the dialog box to automatically add table of contents entries when you export the file as a PDF.

5 In the Styles in Table of Contents area, click on a paragraph style in the Other Styles list, and then click the Add button to move it into the Include Paragraph Styles list. This marks the style so that InDesign can generate a table of contents that includes all paragraphs to which the style is applied. You can add more than one paragraph style.

Styles in Table of Contents

Include Paragraph Styles:

heading1

<< Add

Remove >>

Other Styles:

[No Paragraph Style]

Chapter title

[Basic Paragraph]

toc-entry

toc-title

Style: heading1

Entry Style: toc-entry

Hot tip

If you use the default TOC styles, they are added to the Paragraph Styles panel when you complete the new style process. You can create a Table of Contents style using the InDesign default paragraph styles, and then edit these to suit your purposes at a later stage.

6 To control the appearance of the contents entries, use the Entry Style pop-up in the Style area to choose a paragraph style. Either create your own paragraph style before you begin creating a Table of Contents Style, or select New Paragraph Style from the bottom of the Entry Style pop-up menu to create a paragraph style on the fly. Again, TOC body text, which appears in the list, is a default style created by InDesign. If you have more than one style in the Include Paragraph Styles list, click on each in turn and choose a formatting style from the Entry Style pop-up.

7 Click the OK button when you are satisfied with your settings, to return to the Table of Contents Styles dialog box. OK this dialog box to complete the setup process.

Creating a Table of Contents

When you have applied paragraph styles throughout the document to elements such as titles and subheads that you want to include in a table of contents, and you have created a Table of Contents Style, you can proceed to generate the table of contents.

 Choose Layout>Table of Contents. If you have set up more than one Table of Contents style, make sure you choose the appropriate style from the TOC Style pop-up menu. The Table of Contents dialog box displays the same settings as the ones you set up when you initially created the TOC style.

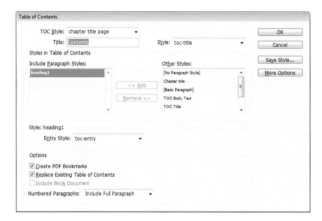

 At this stage, you can adjust any of the settings to create a custom Table of Contents style based on the settings initially displayed. This does not change the specifications of the Style – just this instance.

 Click OK to generate the table of contents as a new text file. Use the Loaded text cursor to place the table of contents into an existing text frame, or press and drag the cursor to define the width and height of a new contents frame.

 If you used the default TOC paragraph styles you can edit them to format the table of contents as required.

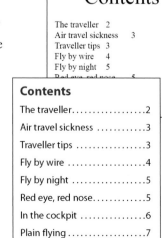

182

5 A table of contents becomes out of date if you make changes in the document that affect content entries. To regenerate a table of contents, choose Layout>Table of Contents. This takes you back into the Table of Contents dialog box. In the Options area, select the Replace Existing Table of Contents checkbox; then click OK. A message box appears to indicate that the table of contents has been updated. Click OK. InDesign regenerates the table of contents and flows it back into the existing table of contents text frame.

6 To generate a table of contents for an entire book, make sure you have the Book panel visible, with the correct book tab selected. When you create a table of contents for a book, you may well locate the table of contents in its own InDesign document with other front matter such as disclaimers and copyright statements. Working in the document where you want to locate the table of contents, choose Layout>Table of Contents. Select the required table of contents style from the TOC Style pop-up; then check that all other settings are what you require. Make sure that the Include Book Document checkbox in the Options area is selected; then click OK to generate the table of contents text file.

Creating an Index Entry

To create an index, you first need to create the individual index entry references; then you can generate the index as a new text file, which you can format and edit to meet your requirements.

1. To create an index entry, choose Window>Type & Tables>Index (Shift+F8), to show the Index panel if it is not already showing. Working with the Type tool, click to place the Text insertion point, or highlight the word or words you want to include in the index entry.

must roam to fulfil a wanderlust that will eventually lead us home. Astronauts on the other hand are a world apart; separated from the daily footsteps that unite and

2. In the Index panel, click the Reference mode button to create index entries for the index. (Click the Topic mode button to create topics in the index.)

3. Choose New Page Reference from the Index panel menu (▾☰), or click the Create a New Index Entry button (▭) at the bottom of the Index panel.

4. The highlighted word appears in the Level 1 text field of the New Page Reference dialog box.

5. Choose a page numbering option for the index reference from the Type pop-up list. This option determines what page number or page number range appears with the index reference.

6 Click OK to add the page reference to the Index panel.

7 Repeat the above process for every word you want to include in the index.

Viewing and Managing Index Entries

Use the Index panel to check, manage and edit the index as you continue to work on it.

1 Click the expand/ collapse triangle to show/hide the index entries in each alphabetic section. Alphabetic sections that do not contain index entries do not have an expand/collapse triangle.

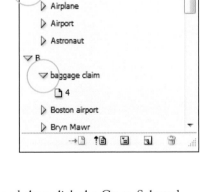

2 Click the expand/ collapse button for an index entry to show/ hide its page number reference.

3 Click a page number reference entry in the panel, and then click the Go to Selected Marker button ( ), at the bottom of the panel, to scroll the page and position the Text insertion point at the index entry marker in the text.

4 Choose Update Preview from the Index panel menu, or click the Update Preview button ( ) to update information in the Index panel. You may need to do this, for example, if you have made edits to the text that result in index entry markers moving to different pages.

5 Working in Reference mode, double-click either an index entry, or the index entry page reference, to edit settings in the Page Reference Options dialog box.

Hot tip

Index markers, visible when you choose Type>Show Hidden Characters, are inserted in the text when you create an index entry:

Once upon Astronauts

If you delete the index marker, the index reference is removed from the Index panel.

Hot tip

To delete an index entry, click on the entry in the Index panel to select it; then click the Wastebasket icon at the bottom of the panel.

Beware

Only begin to structure and build your index when the text content is unlikely to change very much. If you start working on your index too early, changes, such as deleting chunks of text, may affect indexing you have already done.

Generating an Index

At various stages as you build an index you will probably need to generate the index, in a text frame, to check and print it.

Hot tip

If you are generating an index for an entire book, in a separate index document, make sure that you include the index document itself in the book list.

1 To create an index, choose Generate Index from the Index panel menu, or click the Generate Index button ( ) at the bottom of the panel.

2 In the Generate Index dialog box, change the title from Index if you want different wording for the title of your index. Use the Title Style pop-up list to choose a paragraph style to specify the appearance of the title.

Hot tip

See page 50 for further information on placing text files.

3 Click OK. InDesign generates the index as a new text file and displays the Loaded text cursor. Use standard InDesign techniques to place the index text file. InDesign automatically generates paragraph styles (Index Level 1, Index Section Head, and Index Title), and uses these to format the index. If you have a multi-level index, InDesign generates Index Level 2 and 3 styles as well. You can edit these automatically generated styles, if necessary, to specify the exact appearance of the index.

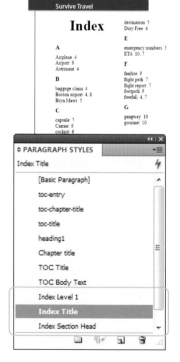

Hot tip

To work with index entries for all documents included in a book, click the Book checkbox at the top of the Index panel.

To generate an index for an entire book, make sure you select the Include Book Documents checkbox in the Generate Index dialog box:

☑ Replace Existing Index
☑ Include Book Documents
☐ Include Entries on Hidden Layers

4 To regenerate an index after you make document changes that affect existing index entries, choose Generate Index from the panel menu. Make sure that the Replace Existing Index checkbox is selected, and then click OK.

Creating a Book

Use the Book panel to bring together a series of individual (but related) InDesign documents, such as the chapters of a book or technical manual, so that you can easily manage page numbering across the entire book, as well as create and maintain consistency of styles and color swatches. You can also create a table of contents and index for all documents included in a book list.

A book file has one style source document. The style source document is used to synchronize styles and colors to ensure consistency throughout the book.

Don't forget

If you want the Book panel to automatically create sections at the start of each document in order to number pages in the book sequentially, set up automatic page numbering in each individual document you add to the book.

① To create a new book file, choose File>New>Book.

② Navigate to the folder where you want to save the book, using standard Windows/Mac techniques. Enter a name for the book: the extension for a book is ".indb". Click Save.

| File name: | travel guide .indb | ▼ |
| Save as type: | Book | ▼ |

③ The Book panel appears on screen. The name of your book appears as a tab in the Book panel. You can have multiple book files open at the same time. You can now start adding InDesign documents to the book. Documents you add do not need to be open to include them in the book list.

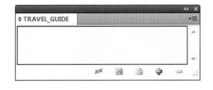

④ To add an InDesign document to the book list, either click the Add document button ( ) at the bottom of the panel, or choose Add Document from the Book panel menu (▾≡).

Add Document...

Replace Document...

Remove Document

Save Book

Save Book As...

Close Book

Preflight Book...

Package Selected Documents For Print...

Export Book to EPUB...

Export Selected Documents to PDF...

Print Selected Documents...

⑤ Navigate to the file you want to add. Select it; then click Open. The file name appears in the book list. A page range for the document

Hot tip

Use a template as the starting point for each document you include in a book. This ensures consistency from the outset for elements such as page size, margins, columns, and master page objects, as well as styles and swatches.

Use the Synchronize feature in the Book panel to ensure that changes you make to styles and swatches are implemented consistently across the book.

...cont'd

appears to the right of the entry in the book list. The first document you add becomes the style source. You can change the style source at any time (see page 190 for further information).

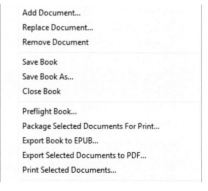

6 Continue to add documents to the book list until the book is complete. Provided that they are in the same folder, you can select more than one file at a time to add to the book list.

7 If you have multiple books open in the Book panel, choose Close Book from the panel menu to close the active book only. To close all books, click the Close button in the Book panel title bar.

8 You can save changes that you make to a book list (for example if you add or delete documents in the list) by choosing Save Book from the Book panel menu.

9 To print documents in a book, select the documents you want to print and then choose Print Selected Documents from the Book panel menu, or click the Print Book button (🖨) at the bottom of the panel. To print the entire book, click in the blank area at the bottom of the panel so that no individual documents are selected, and then choose Print Book from the panel menu, or click the Print Book button.

Managing a Book

There is a variety of ways in which you can manage and edit a book list when preparing the publication.

① To open a document, double-click on the document name in the Book panel. An open document icon ( ) appears to the right of the file entry.

② To change the order of the documents in your book list, drag a document name up or down in the list. Page numbering updates automatically for all documents affected by the move.

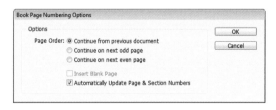

③ To remove a document, click on the document name to select it; then choose Remove Document from the panel menu, or click the Remove Documents button (⊑) at the bottom of the panel. Removing a file from the book list does not close the document if it is open.

④ In a book, automatic page numbering is on by default. When you add, remove or reorder documents,

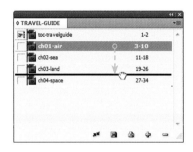

numbering updates automatically so that pages remain numbered sequentially. This also happens if you add or remove pages within documents that are part of a book. To turn off automatic pagination, choose Book Page Numbering Options from the Panel menu; then deselect the Automatically Update Page & Section Numbers checkbox.

⑤ To save changes to the structure or content of the book list, click the Save Book button (🖫), or choose Save Book from the panel menu.

Hot tip

An alert icon (⚠) appears to the right of a document's page range in the Book panel to indicate a document that has been modified while the panel was closed. Double-click the document name to open the file and to update the Book panel.

Hot tip

A question mark icon to the right of a document's page range indicates a moved, renamed or deleted document:

To relink to a missing document, click on the document name to select it; then choose Replace Document from the Book panel menu. Navigate to the missing file, click on it to select it, and then click the Open button.

Synchronizing a Book

A book file has one style source document. The style source is the master file that is used to update other book files to ensure consistency of styles and colors when you synchronize the book. The first document you add to the book panel automatically becomes the style source, indicated by the Style Source icon that appears in the left-hand column of the Book panel, next to the file name entry.

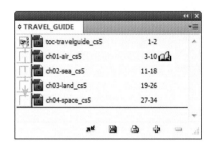

Don't forget

A question mark icon
(❓) to the right of a document's page range indicates a moved, renamed or deleted document. Click on the document name to select it; then choose Replace Document from the Book panel menu to relink to a missing document.

 ① To change the style source status to another document in the list, click the Style Source box in the column to the left of the document icon. The Style Source icon moves to the file. There can be only one style source file in a book.

Don't forget

Use the Synchronize command to copy styles and color swatches from the style source document to the selected documents in the Book panel.

Styles or color swatches with identical names are updated in the selected documents to match the style source. You can use the Synchronize Options dialog box to control which sets of attributes are copied.

Styles and swatches in the style source that are not present in the selected documents are added to them.

Styles and swatches in the selected documents that are not in the style source are left unchanged.

② To synchronize all documents in the book list to the style source document, make sure that none of the documents in the book list is selected. To do this, either click in the blank area of the Book panel below the list of documents, or hold down Ctrl/Command and click any selected documents in the list. Choose Synchronize Book from the Book panel menu, or click the Synchronize button (🔲) at the bottom of the panel.

③ To synchronize specific documents to the style source, select the documents; then choose Synchronize Selected Documents from the Book panel menu, or click the Synchronize button.

④ To control which settings you synchronize, select Synchronize Options from the panel menu. Click the checkboxes to deselect any settings you do not want to synchronize.

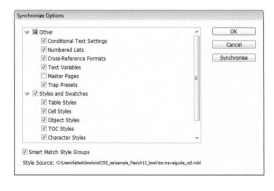

14 Printing and Exporting

Printing a Composite

When you print a composite, all colors or shades in the document are printed on one sheet of paper. Printing from InDesign follows standard Windows and Mac principles.

① To print a composite proof, choose File>Print. Select your printer from the Printer pop-up menu. Enter the number of copies you want to print. In the Pages area, make sure the All

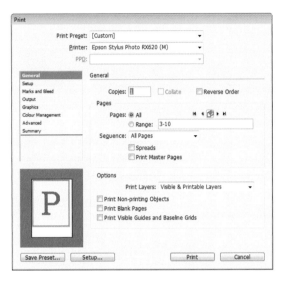

Pages radio button is selected to print all pages in the document, or click the Range button to print specific pages. Enter the page numbers you want to print in the Range entry field. To specify a continuous range of pages, enter numbers separated by a hyphen, e.g. 10-15. To specify individual pages, enter numbers separated by a comma, e.g. 3, 6, 12. You can combine both techniques, e.g. 1-4, 8, 10, 12-15.

② Select checkboxes in the Options area as required if you want to print page elements that do not normally print:

non-printing objects, blank pages or non-printing guides. Use the Print Layers pop-up to control which layers print.

③ Click printing categories in the categories list to create settings for each in turn. Select the Setup category to set options for Paper Size, Orientation and Scale. As you make changes to these settings, the Preview area updates to give a visual preview of how the InDesign page will print on the selected paper size. Keeping an eye on the Preview can save you from printing with inappropriate settings. If the page size of your document is larger than the paper size you want to

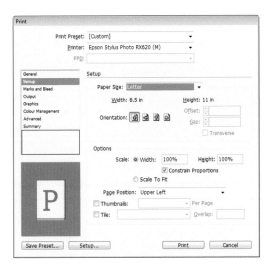

print on, you can use the Scale to Fit option. InDesign scales the page, and any printer's marks and bleed, to fit onto the selected paper size.

4. Marks and Bleeds are used by commercial printers when preparing pages for the press, but you can also use marks and bleed settings when printing composite proof copies of your pages. For example, you might sometimes print using Crop Marks so that you can trim a page to its final cut page size

Marks and Bleed

Marks

☐ All Printer's Marks
☐ Crop Marks
☐ Bleed Marks
☐ Registration Marks
☐ Color Bars
☐ Page Information

Typ**e:** Default
Weight: 0.25 pt
Offset: 0p6

Bleed and Slug

☑ Use Document Bleed Settings
Bleed:

Top: 1p0   Left: 1p0
Bottom: 1p0   Right: 1p0

☐ Include Slug Area

for proofing purposes. Bear in mind that if you select any of the Marks and Bleed options, these add to the overall size of the printed area and, as a result, not all page marks and bleed objects may fit on your chosen page size.

5. In the Output category, leave the Color pop-up set to Composite RGB to print a color composite proof. Select Composite Gray to

Output

Color: Composite RGB   ☐ Text as Black
Trapping:
Flip: ☐ Negative
Screening:

...cont'd

Beware

If you import transparency effects into your document, or use the Effects panel, you need to consider which Transparency Flattener setting to use. To print transparent effects, InDesign divides overlapping areas into discrete segments, which are output as either vector or rasterized areas. The transparency flattener setting controls the balance between vector and bitmap (rasterized) information used to output these transparent areas.

Always advise your printer or service provider that you are using transparent effects in InDesign and ask for their recommendation as to which Flattener preset you should choose.

print a grayscale version of the document. If you are printing to a PostScript output device, you can choose Separations from the Color pop-up. You can then control advanced output settings such as Trapping, halftone screen settings and which inks print.

6 In the Images area of the Graphics category, the Send Data pop-up menu allows you to choose quality settings for images in your document. Leave this on Optimized

Subsampling for a basic composite proof. For a PostScript printer, you may need to download fonts to the printer if you have used fonts in the document that are not resident on the printer itself. Leave the download pop-up set to Complete.

7 In the Advanced category, choose a Transparency Flattener setting from the Preset pop-up if you have used Transparency or any effects such as Drop Shadow and Feathering from the Effects panel.

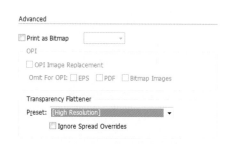

8 Click the Setup button to access the printer's own print settings dialog box. InDesign displays a warning box,

which recommends that where possible you use settings from the InDesign Print dialog box, rather than from the printer's dialog box. Refer to your printer's instruction manual for information on the options available with your printer.

9 Click Print when you are satisfied with your settings.

Hot tip

Print service providers can find further information on transparency output issues on the Print Service Provider Resource pages of the Adobe Solutions Network website.

Live Preflight

Preflighting a document, before handing it off to a service provider or printer, typically consists of checking for problems such as unwanted spot colors, images in the wrong color mode, overmatter and so forth, that might cause unwanted results or problems at output. The task is typically carried out as part of a final checking process, often by trained pre-press professionals.

InDesign CS4 and CS5 can perform a continuous "live" preflight as you create, edit and manipulate a document. You can set the conditions that constitute a "problem" and Live Preflight alerts you with a red circle in the Preflight readout at the bottom of the InDesign window when it detects problems.

The Preflight Panel

Use the Preflight panel to specify which Preflight Profile you want to use in a document and to find and fix problems identified by the profile.

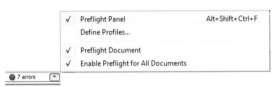

1 To specify a Preflight Profile for the active document, use the Live Preflight pop-up menu to choose Preflight Panel, or choose Window>Output>Preflight (Ctrl/Com+Alt+Shift+F).

2 Make sure that the On checkbox is selected

3 Use the Profile switcher pop-up menu to specify the preflight profile you want to use to check the document. As soon as you choose a new profile InDesign starts checking the document, indicated by the readout in the bottom left corner of the dialog box. If there are errors in the document a red circle indicates this, along with a readout of the total number of errors. Errors are listed, by category, in the Error pane.

Creating Preflight Profiles

InDesign automatically applies the [Basic] preflight profile to new and converted documents.

InDesign CS3 does not have Live Preflight functionality. You can use File>Preflight to perform a more limited set of preflight checks.

Hot tip

Click on the Live Preflight pop-up triangle, along the bottom edge of the InDesign window to reveal the Live Preflight pop-up menu. Use the menu to switch Live Preflight on/ off for the active document only, or all documents.

Don't forget

Live Preflight is switched on by default. The Live Preflight function can check for a wide range of conditions such as missing files or fonts, out of date files, images with the wrong color space and overset text amongst others.

Hot tip

You can also use the Live Preflight pop-up menu to access the Preflight panel and the Preflight Profiles dialog box.

① To define a new profile, with the Profiles panel visible, choose Define Profile from the panel menu. Alternatively, click the Preflight Menu pop-up triangle, then select Define Profiles.

② Click the New Preflight Profile button (⊞) on the left of the Preflight Profiles dialog box to begin creating a new profile. Enter a name for the new profile in the Profile Name entry box, replacing the highlighted placeholder name. The new name appears in the profiles list on the left of the dialog box.

③ Use the Expand triangle (▷) to show options for each of the categories. There are six categories. Switch on the options you want to identify as problems as required.

Examine and fix problems

① Problems identified in the document are listed by category in the Error pane of the Preflight panel. Click the Expand/Collapse triangle to the left of a category or sub-category to reveal specific problems identified.

② Click on a problem in the list to select it. If necessary, click the Info expand triangle to display the info area of the panel. An explanation of the problem for the selected entry appears in the info area, with a suggested solution.

③ Click the hyperlink page number to the right of the entry in the Error pane to move to and highlight the specific problem in the document so that you can examine the issue and make decisions about how to fix it.

Package

The Package command is useful when you are preparing to send a document to your printer or service bureau. Packaging facilitates the process of bringing together the InDesign document and all image files and fonts used in the document – copying them into a folder, which you can then send.

Hot tip

To create a package for a Book publication you must choose Package Book from the Book panel menu. If you have selected individual documents in the Book panel, you can choose Package Selected Documents.

1 Choose File>Package. You get a warning alert indicated by a warning triangle in the Package dialog box summary if InDesign detects any potential

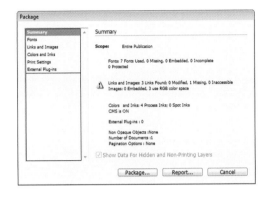

problems. You can either continue with the packaging, or cancel the Package dialog box and use the Preflight panel to locate and resolve issues with the document.

2 If you click Package, the Printing Instructions box appears. Use this, if necessary, to supply contact details and any specific printing instructions to the printer. The

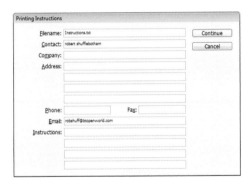

Printing Instructions are saved into the package folder as a plain text file that can be opened by any text editing application. Click the Continue button.

Hot tip

To get more detailed information on aspects of the package, click the categories on the left of the Package dialog box.

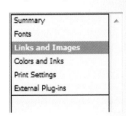

3 In the Package Publication dialog box, specify where you want to save the package folder, and specify the name for the package folder in the Folder Name entry box.

4 Select options to specify the set of items to be copied into the package folder.

...cont'd

Copy Fonts (Except CJK) – copies the fonts required to print the document to a folder named "Document fonts" in the package folder.

Copy Linked Graphics – is an important option, as the original image file holds the complete file information needed for high- resolution printing. If you do not copy linked graphics to the folder, the document will print using low-resolution screen versions of images – typically producing poor-quality results. InDesign automatically creates a sub-folder named "Links" within the package folder when you select this option.

Update Graphic Links in Package – allows InDesign to rewrite the paths of links to the images it copies to the Links folder.

Use Document Hyphenation Exceptions Only – prevents the document from composing with the external user dictionary on the computer which opens the file. It can be important to select this option when sending the document to a printer/service bureau.

⑤ Click the Package button to start the process of copying files as necessary to the package folder. The Font Alert appears to remind you about copyright of fonts. Click OK if you are satisfied that you are not breaking any copyright

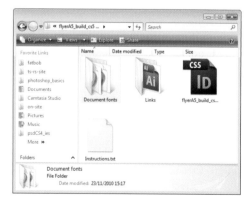

agreements for the fonts in the document. InDesign gathers the files into the specified folder.

Exporting to PDF

You can export an InDesign document as PDF (Portable Document Format), either for high-resolution printing, or for viewing using Acrobat Reader or Web browsers. This section examines how you export documents for on-screen viewing.

One major advantage of using PDF format is that it preserves the layout and content of the original InDesign document without the viewer needing to have access to InDesign itself. The other advantage is the small file sizes that PDF offers.

Hot tip

To get the best results when you view a PDF file exported from InDesign, use Acrobat reader 6.0 or later.

1. To export a file in PDF format, finalize your layouts and save the file. Choose File>Export. Choose Adobe PDF (Print) from the Save as type pop-up (Windows), or Format pop-up (Mac). Specify a location where you want to save the file, using standard Windows/Mac techniques. Enter a name for the file, and then click Save.

2. In the Export PDF dialog box, select an option from the Adobe PDF Preset pop-up menu. Each preset specifies a set of predefined settings, optimized for a particular PDF output requirement. For example, [Press Quality] is intended for PDF files that will be printed on imagesetters or platesetters as high-quality final output. [Press Quality] typically preserves the maximum amount of information contained in the original InDesign document. [Smallest File Size], on the other hand, creates PDF files that are suitable for on-screen

viewing, for example on the World Wide Web. [Smallest File Size] downsamples image quality and compresses file information to create a file that is as small as possible. When you choose

Hot tip

To import a PDF Preset supplied to you by your printer or output bureau, choose File>Adobe PDF Presets>Define. In the Adobe PDF Presets dialog box, click the Load button, and then navigate to the Presets file. Click on the Presets file to select it, and then click Open:

199

...cont'd

Hot tip

If you are preparing PDFs for commercial printing, check with your printer or output bureau about which Compatibility and Standard settings to use.

Beware

Select the Spreads checkbox if you want left- and right-hand pages to be downloaded as a single spread. Use this option so that the PDF viewer displays spreads as if you are reading a magazine or book. Do not select the Spreads option for print publishing, as this can prevent your commercial printer from imposing the pages.

Don't forget

After you choose a preset, if you select a category from the list on the left, and then make changes to the predefined settings, "(modified)" is appended to the preset name.

one of the presets, settings in the PDF export categories change according to the preset you choose.

③ In the General category, specify whether you want to export all the pages in the document, or a specified range of pages. In the Options area, select the View PDF After Exporting checkbox, to launch the default PDF viewer, typically Acrobat Reader, so that you can check the result.

④ Compression settings are controlled initially by the preset you choose. Again it is important if you are preparing a PDF for commercial printing that you consult with your printer or output

bureau about which preset to choose, and only make changes to compression settings as directed.

⑤ You typically do not need to create Marks and Bleeds settings for PDFs intended for on-screen viewing. For PDFs intended for print, ask your printer or output bureau about the options you should set to meet their printing specifications.

6 In the Output category settings, if you are using the [Smallest File Size] preset, leave Color options set to the defaults.

Hot tip

Your commercial printer or output bureau may well have a PDF Preset that they can supply, which defines PDF export specifications to meet their specific requirements.

7 In the Advanced category, for printed final output, and depending on the Compatibility setting you are using, the Transparency Flattener setting can be important; it can affect the quality of printed output if you have used effects such as Drop Shadow, Feathering or Opacity from the Effects panel. Always inform your printer the first time you use a new transparency effect, and check with them as to which Flattener setting you should choose.

Hot tip

If required, choose Security from the categories list. Use the Security settings to control the degree of access that a viewer has for the PDF file. For example, you can set a Document Open Password so that only viewers who know the password are able to view the file. In the Permissions area, you can select the Use a password… checkbox to control editing and printing rights for the PDF.

8 Click Export when you are satisfied with the settings. If you chose the View PDF after Export option in the General category, Acrobat Reader launches and displays the exported PDF file.

Saving a Preset

If you use a custom set of PDF settings on a regular basis it is worth creating your own preset.

1 To create a PDF preset, apply the settings you want in each of the PDF Export categories. Click the Save Preset button. Enter a name for the preset in the Save Preset dialog box, and click OK. The custom preset is now available in the Presets pop-up menu.

Don't forget

When you create PDF settings and then export the PDF file, the settings you created remain in force for other InDesign documents until you change them again.

Export for Dreamweaver

The Export for Dreamweaver command is a fast, convenient way to repurpose InDesign content for use on the Web.

 Start by selecting the text and picture frames you want to export to XHTML/Dreamweaver.

Choose File>Export for>Dreamweaver. In the Save as dialog box, specify the folder where you want to save the content. If you are exporting images, InDesign sets up a web-images folder within the folder you specify – and then saves optimized copies of images in the InDesign document to this location.

Enter a name for the file. Leave the Save as Type pop-up menu (Windows), or Format pop-up (Mac), set to All Files. Click Save.

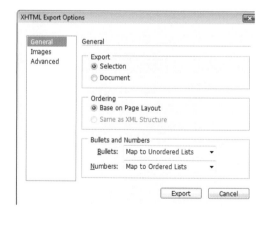

In the XHTML Export Options dialog box, with the General category selected, specify whether you want to export selected objects, or the entire document. You can also convert Numbered and Bullet lists to their equivalents – ordered or unordered lists – in XHTML.

Click on the Images category to control how images are exported. Leave the Copy Images pop-up set to Optimized to export a copy of the original image optimized for web viewing according to the GIF and JPEG optimization settings you select. Leave Image Conversion set to Automatic to allow InDesign to select the best optimization settings automatically, depending on the image type.

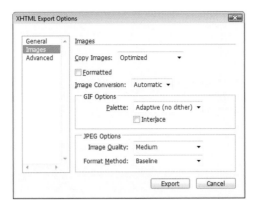

6 Click Advanced in the category list. For CSS Options, select the Empty CSS Declarations radio button if you want InDesign to create an internal style sheet, with empty style declarations for you to complete. Select External CSS if you know the location of a .css file you want to link to.

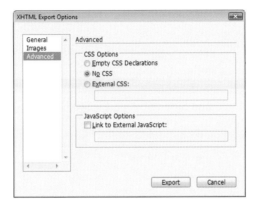

7 Click the Export button. You can then open the exported .html file in Dreamweaver or any other HTML editor to further prepare the exported code for display as a web page.

Hot tip

Select the Formatted checkbox to export images and include effects such as drop shadows applied in InDesign.

Hot tip

Select the Link to External JavaScript checkbox and enter a path to run a JavaScript when the page opens in a browser.

Beware

After you export to XHTML you still need to do some work in Dreamweaver or another HTML editor to create finished web pages.

Snippets

A snippet is an XML file that represents content from an InDesign page. For example, you could save a series of headline, intro and body frames representing a magazine news story as a snippet.

You can easily re-use snippets in other pages or other documents.

Saving Snippets

1 To create a snippet, use the Selection tool to select a single frame or multiple frames.

Rope pumps could save thousands of lives within less than 2 months

2 Choose File>Export. Select InDesign Snippet from the Save as type pop-up (Windows), or Format pop-up (Mac).

3 Enter a name for the file; then click the Save button. Snippets save with an ".idms" file extension.

Adding Snippets to a Document

1 To add a snippet to a document, choose File>Place. Use standard Windows/Mac dialog box techniques to navigate to the snippet you want to place. If necessary, choose InDesign Snippet from the Files of type pop-up. Select the snippet name; then click the Open button, or double-click on the file name.

File name: ecofriendly-03-p3.idms

Files of type: InDesign Snippet

2 Position the loaded cursor then click. The snippet appears on the page with formatting, structure and content exactly as it was exported. Paragraph, Character and Object styles together with color swatches applied to the original objects are also imported.

15 Transformations and Transparency

This chapter introduces the transformation tools. It also shows you how to change objects by adjusting transparency and by applying effects.

The Rotate Tool

The Rotate tool, like the Scale and Skew tools, works around a reference point – the point around which the transformation takes place. The reference point marker appears when you have a selected object and you then click on the Rotate tool. You can reposition the reference point marker if necessary.

1 To rotate an object, first select it with the Selection tool. Click on the Rotate tool. As soon as you select the Rotate tool, the reference point marker ( ) appears on the object. The initial position of the marker is determined by the proxy reference point currently selected in the Control or Transform panel. Position the rotate cursor slightly away from the reference point marker; then drag in a circular direction. Hold down Shift as you drag to constrain the rotation to increments of 45°.

2 To reposition the reference point marker, with the Rotate tool selected, position your cursor on the marker; then drag it to another position. Alternatively, position your cursor at a different location, and then click. You can reposition the marker inside the selected object or anywhere on the page outside it.

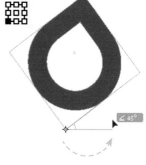

3 To rotate using the Rotate dialog box, select an object using the Selection tool; then double-click the Rotate tool. Enter a rotation amount in the Angle entry field. Enter a value from -360 to 360. Negative values rotate an object in a clockwise direction; positive values act counterclockwise. This rotates the object and its contents.

④ Click the Copy button instead of the OK button to create a rotated copy of the original object.

⑤ You can also use the Rotate field in the Control panel to rotate objects, or the contents of graphic frames.

⑥ To rotate the contents of a graphic frame, first select the content using the Direct Selection tool, then apply the rotation using the Rotate tool, the Rotate dialog box or the Rotate field in the Control panel.

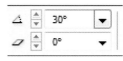

⑦ You can use the Rotate dialog box to create a circular rotation effect. To create this effect it is best to create a vertical and a horizontal ruler guide so that you can work easily around a center point. Start by creating the shape you want to rotate. Position it on the vertical guide above the center point. Make sure the shape remains selected. Select the Rotate tool. Position your cursor where the vertical and horizontal ruler guides meet. Hold down Alt/option, and click. This does two things: it sets the reference point where you click, and it opens the Rotate dialog box. Enter a rotation angle, and then click the Copy button. Make sure the rotated object remains selected; then choose Object>Transform Again>Transform Again to repeat the transformation. Use the same command to continue repeating the transformation.

In InDesign CS5 to quickly rotate a selected object, position your cursor just outside the corner of the object. When the cursor changes to the rotate cursor (↰) drag in a circular direction.

Hot tip

For this technique to work effectively, you need to enter a rotation angle that divides into 360°, for example 15, 30, 36 or 60:

In InDesign CS5 the Rotate, Scale and Shear tools are located in the Free Transform tool group:

The Scale Tool

You can scale objects manually using the Scale tool, or you can use the Scale dialog box. Like the Rotate and Skew tools, the Scale tool scales around a reference point.

1 To scale an object manually using the Scale tool, first select the object with the Selection tool. Then select the Scale tool. The reference point marker appears on the object or group. The position of the marker is determined by the currently selected proxy reference point in the Control or Transform panel. (See page 38 for information on controlling the position of the reference point marker.)

2 Position the Scale cursor slightly away from the reference point marker; then start to drag. To scale the object in proportion, hold down Shift and start to drag at an angle of 45°. To scale the object horizontally only, hold down Shift and drag the cursor horizontally. To scale the object vertically only, hold down Shift and drag the cursor vertically.

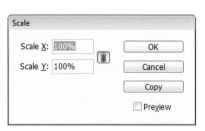

3 To scale an object using the Scale dialog box, select the object using the Selection tool; then double-click the Scale tool. Make sure the Constrain Proportions button is selected; then enter a Scale X or Y amount to scale the object in proportion. Deselect the Constrain Proportions button and enter Scale X or Y values to scale non-proportionally.

Hot tip

To scale the object, but not its contents, use the Direct Selection tool to select all the anchor points in the path; then apply the scaling:

The Shear Tool

Use the Shear tool to slant or shear an object. The Shear tool obeys the same basic principles as the Rotate and Scale tools.

1 To Shear an object manually, first select the object with the Selection tool, and then select the Shear tool. The reference point marker appears on the object or group. The position of the marker is determined by the currently selected proxy reference point in the Control or Transform panel. (See page 38 for information on controlling the position of the reference point marker.)

2 Position the Shear cursor slightly away from the reference point marker, and start to drag. Hold down the Shift key and drag at a 45° angle to constrain the shear. Hold down the Alt/ option key as you shear to create a copy of the original object or group. You can use this technique to create shadow-like effects on objects.

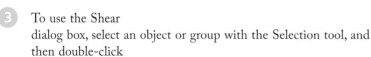

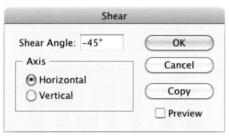

3 To use the Shear dialog box, select an object or group with the Selection tool, and then double-click the Shear tool. Enter a Shear Angle and select Horizontal or Vertical for the shear axis.

Shear	
Shear Angle: -45°	OK
Axis	Cancel
● Horizontal	Copy
○ Vertical	☐ Preview

The Free Transform Tool

Unlike the Rotate, Scale and Skew tools, the Free Transform tool does not display a reference point marker on the selected object when you select the tool. Using the Free Transform tool you can move, scale, rotate, reflect and shear objects. The tool's functionality is very similar to that of the equivalent tool in Photoshop and Illustrator.

1. To scale an object using the Free Transform tool, first select the object using the Selection tool; then select the Free Transform tool. Drag any selection handle to scale the object. Hold down Shift and drag a corner handle to scale the object in proportion. Hold down Alt/option and drag a handle to scale the object around its center point.

2. To rotate a selected object, select the Free Transform tool; then position your cursor slightly outside the object's bounding box. The cursor changes to the rotate cursor. Drag the cursor in a circular direction.

3. To reflect a selected object, select the Free Transform tool; then drag a handle through the opposite edge or handle.

4. To shear a selected object, select the Free Transform tool, start to drag any of the center side or center top handles, but not a corner handle, and then hold down Ctrl/Command as you continue to drag. Use the Shift key as you perform this procedure to constrain the effect. If you copy an object, reflect it and shear it, you can produce some interesting results.

In InDesign CS3 and CS4, when you transform an object with the Free Transform tool, a wireframe representation indicates the result as you drag the mouse. The transformation is applied when you release the mouse:

In CS5 you get a live preview as you drag the mouse.

Transparency and Blending

Using transparency settings, you can allow underlying objects to show through other objects. You can apply transparency to selected objects, including graphic and text frames. You cannot apply transparency to individual text characters, but you can apply transparency selectively to an object's fill or stroke if required.

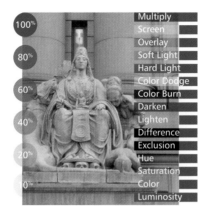

An opacity setting of 100% means that the object is completely solid. An opacity setting of 0% makes an object completely transparent.

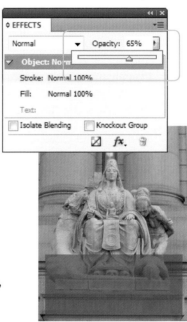

1. To set transparency for an object, select it using the Selection tool. Click the Effects icon if the panel is in the Panel dock, or choose Window>Effects (Ctrl/Command+Shift+F10) to show the Effects panel if it is not already showing.

2. Either drag the Opacity slider, or enter an Opacity amount. The lower the setting, the more transparent an object becomes.

3. To overlay text on a faded, or knocked-back, area of an image, make sure you reduce the opacity for the fill of the text frame, so that the opacity setting is not applied to the text.

This is a caption placed on top of an image. The text frame has a reduced opacity setting.

211

Hot tip

You can also apply blend modes, such as Multiply and Color Burn, to objects using the Blend Mode pop-up menu in the Effects panel. When you apply a blend mode to an object which overlaps other objects the color in the blend object mixes with the colors in the underlying object to produce a different color determined by the blend mode.

Hot tip

To change Opacity or Blend Mode selectively for either the stroke, fill or text of a selected object, make sure you select the appropriate Stroke, Fill or Text entry in the Effects panel before you change settings:

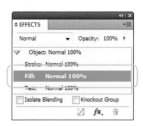

Effects

Used well, Effects can add visual impact and bring a new level of creative potential to In Design layouts, without the need to resort to equivalent features in Photoshop or Illustrator. Effects such as Drop Shadow or Feathering options involve transparency to achieve the change in appearance.

You can apply an Effect to an entire object, or selectively to fill, stroke, or text in a text frame.

Beware

When you use transparency settings, the Transparency Flattener setting you choose when printing or exporting PDFs can affect the final output.

Hot tip

A small transparency indicator (☐) appears alongside page icons in the Pages panel to indicate that an object on the page has a transparency effect applied to it. In CS4 and CS5 you can control whether or not this icon appears by selecting Panel Options from the Pages panel menu.
You can use the Flattener Preview panel (Window>Output> Flattener Preview) to check for objects that use transparency.

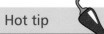

Hot tip

You can also use the Settings For pop-up menu in the Effects dialog box to control where the effect is applied.

1 Click the Effects panel icon, or choose Window>Effects (Shift+Ctrl/Command+F10) to show the Effects panel.

2 Select an object then select Stroke, Fill or Text if you want to apply the effect to a specific attribute of an object, otherwise leave Object selected.

3 Click the Add Effect button (_fx._) at the bottom of the Effects panel. You can also access the Effects menu by clicking the Add Object Effect button in the Control panel.

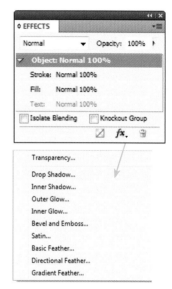

4 Click on the effect you want to apply to access the Effects dialog box.

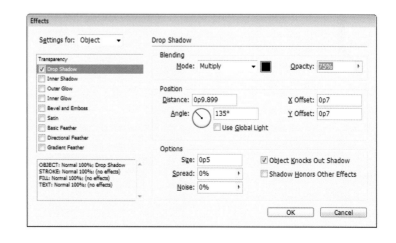

⑤ The object effect you selected from the menu is selected by default and settings available for the effect appear in the dialog box. Clicking in a checkbox switches the default effect on or off. Click on the name of the effect itself to access the controls for that effect.

⑥ Select the Preview checkbox so that you can assess the changes you make to settings on the selected object. When you achieve the result you want, click OK.

⑦ Notice the "fx" icon which indicates that an effect is applied to an object, and whether it is applied to the object, or a specific attribute of the object.

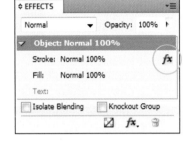

⑧ To edit settings for a selected object double-click on the "fx" icon in the Effects panel.

⑨ To remove all effects applied to a selected object and make it opaque (Opacity = 100%), click the Clear Effects button ( ). You can use commands in the Effects panel menu to clear effects and transparency selectively.

Effects gallery

There are 9 transparency effects available in InDesign:

No effect   Drop Shadow   Inner Shadow   Outer Glow   Inner Glow

Bevel and Emboss   Satin   Basic Feather   Directional Feather   Gradient Feather

213

Beware

Consult with your commercial printer or service bureau when you start to use transparency settings: they can then make any recommendations so that you achieve satisfactory results. If possible, do a test run when you use these features for the first time.

Hot tip

You can apply more than one effect to an object. Click in a checkbox on the left of the Effects dialog box to add more effects. Click the name of the effect to adjust its settings.

Beware

The Effects panel replaces the Transparency palette available in previous versions of InDesign.

Gradient Feather Tool

The Gradient Feather tool provides a quick, convenient technique for applying and controlling one of the most popular InDesign effects – a gradient feather. Apply a gradient feather when you want to gradually fade an object to transparency – this can be a placed image, a group or any InDesign object.

The Gradient Feather tool is not available in InDesign CS3, but you can create equivalent gradient feather effects on an object using the Effects panel, then editing the gradient feather using the Gradient Feather controls in the Effects dialog box. (See pages 212–213 for further information.)

1. Use the Selection tool to select an image, object or group. Select the Gradient Feather tool. Drag across the object to define the length of the fade to transparency and it's angle.

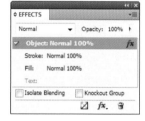

2. In the Effects panel the "fx" icon ( ) indicates that an effect is applied to the object.

Hot tip

To constrain the angle of a gradient feather to vertical, horizontal or increments of 45°, hold down Shift, then drag with the Gradient Feather tool.

3. If you don't achieve the result you want the first time you can simply drag with the Gradient Feather tool again to redefine the effect.

4. To edit the Gradient Effect settings using controls in the Effects dialog box, either double click the fx icon ( ), or click the fx button (fx.) at the bottom of the panel, then choose Gradient Feather.

5. Click the start (▪ – opaque) or end stop (◻ – transparent) on the transparency ramp then drag to control the transition to transparency across the length of the effect defined with the Gradient Feather tool.

Hot tip

Click the Clear All Effects button (▨) at the bottom of the Effects panel to remove all effects from the selected object.

6. For a Linear gradient feather use the Angle dial to control the angle of the feather. Select Radial from the Type pop-up menu to create a gradient feather that fades from the center out.

Gradient Feather

Gradient Stops

Opacity: 100% ▸ Location: 20% ▸

Options

Type: Linear ▾

Angle: 0°

16 Paths and the Pen Tool

The Pen tool group with the Pathfinder commands enables you to create and manipulate the paths of shapes and lines.

Points and Paths

In InDesign, the shape of all basic objects, including frames and shapes drawn with the Pen and Pencil tools, is defined by a path. You can manipulate paths and points in a variety of ways to achieve precisely the shape you need.

Paths and Points

A path consists of two or more anchor points joined together by curve or straight line segments. The Pen tool allows you to position anchor points precisely where you want them as you create the path. You can also control which type of point you create – smooth or corner. The Pencil tool creates freeform paths, which are formed as you drag the cursor.

Open and Closed Paths

Using the Pen and Pencil tools you can create open and closed paths. Objects such as rectangles and ovals, as well as text and graphic frames, are closed paths.

Smooth and Corner Points

There are two kinds of points that you need to understand in order to work creatively and precisely with paths: Smooth points connect two curve segments in a smooth, continuous curve; Corner points allow an abrupt, sharp change in direction at the point. You can create paths consisting of both kinds of points as you draw them, and you can convert points from one type to the other using the Convert Direction Point tool.

Direction Points

When you click on an anchor point connecting curve segments, using the Direct Selection tool, one or two direction points (depending on the type of point) appear, attached to their associated anchor point by direction lines. Direction points control the length of a curve segment and the direction of the curve segment as it leaves the point.

The Pen Tool

The Pen tool is the most versatile and precise tool you can use for defining shapes accurately. Use the Pen tool to create straight line segments, curve segments, or a mixture of both, with precise control over the positioning and type of anchor points.

Straight Line Segments

1 To create a straight line segment, select the Pen tool, position your cursor where you want the line to start, and then click. This sets the first anchor point, and defines the start point of the path.

2 Move the cursor to a new position. (Do not press and drag; simply reposition the cursor.) Click. This sets the second anchor point. A straight line segment is created between the two points. Repeat the procedure to create the number of straight line segments you need.

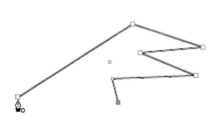

3 To finish drawing the path, position your cursor back at the start point (a small circle appears with the Pen tool cursor), and then click to create a closed path.

4 Alternatively, click the Pen tool again (or any other tool in the Toolbox) to create an open path. Clicking another tool indicates that the path is complete and that you have finished adding segments.

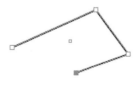

Curve Segments

1 To create curve segments, with the Pen tool selected, position your cursor where you want the path to start. Press and drag. This action sets the first anchor point and defines its associated direction points. (See pages 219–222 for further information on how direction points control the shape of curves.)

(See pages 219–222 for further information on how direction points control the shape of curves.)

Hot tip

Hold down Shift, and click with the Pen tool to constrain straight line segments to horizontal, vertical or increments of 45 degrees.

Hot tip

The center point that appears when you select a path with the Selection tool is not an editable point. It simply indicates the center of the bounding box that represents the outer boundary of the path.

Beware

When you draw an open path with the Pen or Pencil tool, if there is a fill color selected, InDesign attempts to fill the path along an imaginary line from one end point to the other. This can be disconcerting at first. Click the Fill box and then click the None button to prevent this happening.

...cont'd

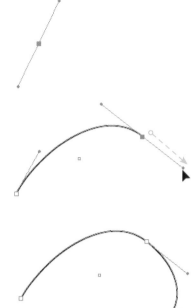

② Release the mouse button.
An anchor point and two
direction points are visible.

③ Move the Pen tool cursor
to a new position. Press
and drag to set another
anchor point and to
define its associated
direction points. Setting
the second anchor point
also defines the curve
segment between the first
and second anchor points.
Repeat the procedure
to create as many curve
segments as you require.

④ To finish drawing the path,
position your cursor back
at the start point (a small
circle appears with the Pen
tool cursor); then click to
create a closed path. Alternatively, click the Pen tool again
(or any other tool) to create an open path.

Adding and deleting points

Using the Add or Delete Anchor Point tools, or the Pen tool, you can
add points to an existing path to achieve the exact shape you require,
and you can delete points from a path to simplify it, if necessary.

① To add an anchor point to a selected path or frame,
select the Add Anchor Point tool, or work with the Pen
tool. Position your cursor on the path; then click to add
a point. Points added to curve segments automatically
appear with direction points. Points added to straight line
segments do not have direction points.

② To delete an existing anchor point, select the path with
either the Selection tool or the Direct Selection tool.
Select the Delete Anchor Point tool, or work with the
Pen tool. Position your cursor on a point; then click to
delete the point. The path redraws without the point.

Selecting and Manipulating Points

To fine-tune the path you are working with you need to select and manipulate anchor points and direction points. Use the Direct Selection tool to work on paths in this way.

Editing Anchor Points

① Use the Direct Selection tool; then click on a path to select it. The path becomes highlighted and the anchor points that form the shape appear as hollow squares. Click on an anchor point to select it. The point becomes solid. If the anchor point connects curve segments, direction points also appear, connected to the anchor point by direction lines. To change the shape of the path, drag the point to a new location.

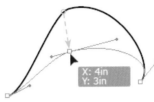

Editing Direction Points

Anchor points on curve segments have associated direction points that control the length and shape of the curve segments. Continue working with the Direct Selection tool to edit direction points.

① To edit the direction points, first select a point that has curve segments entering or leaving it. The anchor point becomes solid and the associated direction points appear, connected to the anchor point by direction lines.

② Position your cursor on a direction point. Drag the direction point further away from the anchor point to increase the length of the curve segment it controls. Drag the direction point closer to the anchor point to make the curve segment shorter.

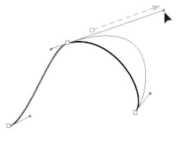

③ Drag a direction point in a circular direction around the anchor point to change the angle at which the curve segment enters or leaves the anchor point. The result is to change the shape of the curve segment.

Hot tip

When you have selected an anchor point using the Direct Selection tool, you can press the Up/Down/Left/Right arrow keys on the keyboard to nudge the points in small steps.

In InDesign CS5 simply hovering over a path with the Direct Selection tool makes the path and it's anchor points available to edit without first clicking to select it.

219

Hot tip

Hold down Shift as you drag anchor and direction points to constrain the movement to vertical, horizontal or multiples of 45°.

In InDesign CS3 and CS4 a preview of the results of an edit appears as a blue line as you drag an anchor or direction point. In CS5 the shape updates immediately as you manipulate it.

Smooth and Corner Points

Understanding the difference between smooth and corner anchor points will give you complete control over the shape of paths.

Smooth Points

A smooth point maintains a smooth, continuous transition or curve from the incoming to the outgoing curve segments, through the anchor point.

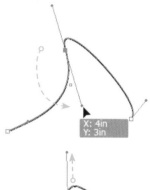

1 Select the Direct Selection tool, then click on a smooth anchor point. Two direction points appear, connected to the anchor point by direction lines. Position your cursor on a direction point; then press and drag in a circular direction around the point. As you move the direction point, the opposite direction point moves like a balance, keeping both direction points perfectly aligned. If you move the direction point further away from or closer to the anchor point, the distance of the opposing direction point does not change.

Corner Points

Use corner points to create a sharp change in direction at the anchor point.

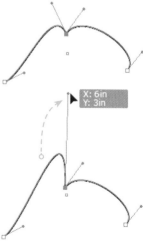

1 Click on a corner point to select it. Two direction points appear, connected to the anchor point by direction lines. Drag a direction point in a circular direction around the anchor point and/or move the direction point closer to or further away from the anchor point. The opposite direction point does not move: for corner points, each direction point works completely independently of the other.

Converting Points and Cutting Paths

The Convert Direction Point tool can convert a smooth point to a corner point and vice versa, and it can also be used to retract direction points or create smooth points.

Converting Smooth to Corner

1. To convert a smooth point to a corner point, select the point using the Direct Selection tool. Select the Convert Direction Point tool. Position your cursor on one of the direction points; then press and drag. The point becomes a corner point – each direction point moves independently of the other.

2. If you are going to make further changes to the direction points to fine-tune the curves, make sure you reselect the Direct Selection tool, rather than continuing to work with the Convert tool.

Converting Corner to Smooth

1. To convert a corner point to a smooth point, select a corner point using the Direct Selection tool. Select the Convert Direction Point tool. Position the cursor on the anchor point (not a direction point); then drag off the point to convert the point to a smooth point and to define the shape of the smooth curve.

2. Reselect the Direct Selection tool to make further changes to the point or direction point. If you continue to work with the Convert tool on the same point, or its direction points, you will undo the results of Step 1.

Hot tip

While working with the Direct Selection tool, you can temporarily access the Convert Direction Point tool by holding down Ctrl/ Command+Alt/option.

Hot tip

You can use the Convert Direction Point techniques on the anchor points that define the shape of a text or graphic frame:

In InDesign CS5, the bottom row of the Pathfinder panel includes buttons for converting points. Choose Window>Object & Layout>Pathfinder to display the panel.

Convert Point:

...cont'd

In InDesign CS4 and CS5, using the Convert Direction Point tool, you can click on a direction point to retract that individual point.

Retracting Direction Points

1. To retract both direction points for either a smooth or a corner point, first select the point with the Direct Selection tool. Select the Convert Direction Point tool. Position your cursor on the anchor point; then click to retract the direction points. The incoming and outgoing curve segments are redrawn accordingly.

Converting a Retracted Point to a Smooth Point

1. To convert a retracted point to a smooth point, select a path with the Direct Selection tool. A retracted point is one that has no direction points associated with it when you click on it with the Direct Selection tool. Select the Convert Direction Point tool. Position your cursor on the retracted point; then drag off the point to create a smooth point and define the shape of the incoming and outgoing curve segments.

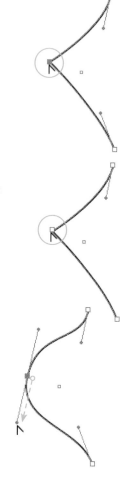

The Scissors Tool

Use the Scissors tool to split or cut a path anywhere along a curve or straight line segment, or at an anchor point.

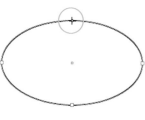

1. To split an open or closed path, select the Scissors tool. Position your cursor at the point on the path where you want to cut it. (The path does not have to be selected, and you do not have to click on an existing anchor point.) Click. Two anchor points are created at the point at which you click.

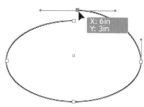

Hot tip

If you split a picture frame containing an image you end up with a copy of the image inside each half of the frame.

Hot tip

After you cut a path, select the Direct Selection tool to make further changes to either side of the cut path if required.

Pathfinder Commands

Use the Pathfinder commands to create new shapes from overlapping frames or shapes. The resultant paths can be interesting, complex shapes that it would be difficult to create any other way.

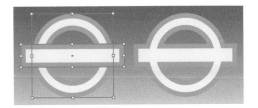

Hot tip

Choose Window>Object & Layout>Pathfinder to show the Pathfinder panel if it is not already showing.

Add

The Add pathfinder command creates a more complex shape from overlapping shapes. Add is useful when you want to create a complex shape with a unified outline or stroke from two or more basic shapes.

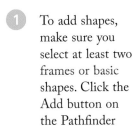

1 To add shapes, make sure you select at least two frames or basic shapes. Click the Add button on the Pathfinder panel, or choose Object>Pathfinder>Add. When frames or shapes have different fill and stroke attributes, the Add command applies the fill and stroke attributes of the frontmost object to the resultant shape.

Don't forget

Typically, the pathfinder commands work by creating new shapes where existing paths overlap.

Subtract

The Subtract command acts like a punch – shapes in front of the backmost object punch through and cut away areas of the backmost object where they overlap. The frontmost objects are deleted when you use the command. This is a useful technique for creating completely transparent areas in a shape.

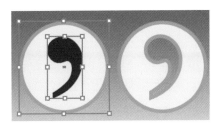

1 To subtract shapes, make sure you select at least two frames or basic shapes. Click the Subtract button on the Pathfinder panel, or choose Object> Pathfinder>Subtract. When frames or shapes have different fill and stroke attributes, the backmost shape retains its fill and stroke attributes when you use the Subtract command.

Don't forget

You must have two overlapping shapes or frames selected to use commands in the Pathfinder panel.

...cont'd

Intersect

The Intersect command creates a new shape where two shapes or frames overlap. Areas that do not overlap are removed. You can use the command for only two objects at a time. If you attempt to apply the command with more than two objects selected, a warning prompt indicates that you cannot proceed.

① To intersect shapes, select two frames or basic shapes, click the Intersect button in the Pathfinder panel, or choose Object> Pathfinder>Intersect. The resultant shape retains the fill and stroke attributes of the frontmost object.

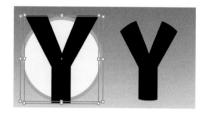

Exclude Overlap

The Exclude Overlap command makes the area where two or more frames or shapes overlap completely transparent.

① To use Exclude Overlap, select two or more frames or basic shapes; then click the Exclude Overlap button in the Pathfinder panel, or choose Object> Pathfinder>Exclude Overlap. The resultant shape retains the fill and stroke attributes of the frontmost object.

Minus Back

Minus Back is the opposite of the Subtract command. Objects behind cut away the frontmost object where they overlap.

① To use Minus Back, select two or more frames or basic shapes; then click the Minus Back button in the Pathfinder panel, or choose Object> Pathfinder> Minus Back. The resultant shape retains the fill and stroke attributes of the frontmost object.

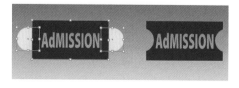

17

Interactive

Choose the Interactive or
Interactive PDF workspace
from the Workspace pop-up
menu to get started with
creating interactive SWF
(Flash Player) and
PDF files.

Animations

It's easy and fun to create animations in InDesign CS5. Using the Animation panel you can apply motion presets to an object and you can edit settings such as the trigger event, speed and duration to customize the animation.

1 To create an animation, position the object you want to animate. Make sure it remains selected. In the Animation panel, enter a name for the animated object.

2 Select an animation type from the Preset pop-up menu. For example, if you want an object to move down the screen to its current position on the page, choose Fly in from Top. The animated object symbol appears in the bottom right of the object (provided that Frame Edges are showing) to indicate that there is an animation applied to it. Also, a green motion preset line appears to indicate the distance and the direction of the animation.

3 To edit the motion path, select the animated object to show the motion path line. Select the Direct Selection tool. Click on the motion path line to select it. The line turns blue. Click once on one of the hollow end points – the end point turns solid to indicate it is selected. Drag the end point to control the distance and angle for the animation.

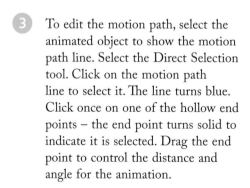

 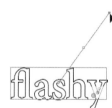
4 Choose an event from the Events pop-up menu. On Page Load is the default – as soon as the page appears on screen the animation will start. There are options to trigger the animation by clicking the mouse on the screen or on the object itself, or when the mouse rolls over the object.

5 If required, specify a duration for the animation, specify the number of times it runs or whether it loops continually.

6 Select an option from the Speed Options pop-up menu to control the speed dynamics of the animation. Ease In/Out options create animations that gather or lose speed across the duration of the animation.

7 Click the Properties expand triangle to access a range of advanced animation controls.

Hot tip

Click the Remove Animation button ( ) in the Animation panel to remove an animation from a selected object.

Preview

You can preview changes in the Preview panel at any point as you create and adjust settings for animations and other interactive features.

1 To preview an animation, either show the Preview panel, or click the Preview button ( ) at the bottom of the Animation, Buttons or Timing panels.

2 Click the Play button to load and play the animation and preview any other interactive features.

Don't forget

Animations do not export to Interactive PDF.

227

3 The three buttons at the bottom right of the Preview panel allow you to specify whether you preview interactive elements for the entire document ( ), for the current page or spread ( ), or for a selected object only ( ). Multi-page documents with substantial use of interactive features take longer to generate a preview; previewing interactivity for a page/spread or object only can save time if you don't need to review and test interactive elements throughout a document.

Hot tip

Make the Preview panel bigger to get a clearer representation of the animation as you review it.

Timing

For objects with an On Page Load or On Page Click event assigned to them, you can use the Timing panel to specify the order in which the animations play. You can also set animations to play simultaneously and you can set a delay for an animation.

1 To change the order in which animations play, select either On Page Load or On Page Click from the Event pop-up menu. Animations in that category appear in the list box.

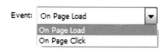

2 Drag an animation name label up or down to change the play order. Animations play in order from top to bottom.

3 To set animations to play at the same time, select more than one animation in the list box, then click the Play Together button. A square bracket appears to the left of animations set to play simultaneously.

4 Select an animation set to play at the same time as another animation, then click the Play Separately button ( ) to treat them as separate entities.

5 To delay the start of an animation, select it in the list box, then enter a delay amount in the delay entry box.

Delay: 3 second

6 For linked animations, select all the linked animations in order to access controls for Play number of times or Loop.

Buttons

Buttons initiate an action when clicked in exported SWF and PDF files and provide a key method for introducing interactivity in interactive SWF and PDF documents. You can drag in ready made buttons from the Sample Buttons panel or you can select an object then convert it to a button in the Buttons panel.

1. To convert a selected object to a button, either choose Object>Interactive>Convert to Button, or click the Convert Object to Button button ( ) at the bottom of the Buttons panel. Controls in the Buttons panel become available for the selected button object.

2. Enter a descriptive name for the button to help indicate its purpose and to distinguish it from other buttons.

3. Select an Event from the Event pop-up menu. PDF only events are indicated. On Release is useful as it allows the user the chance to change their mind and slide their cursor off an option without triggering the event.

4. Select an action from the Actions pop-up menu. (SWF and PDF only actions are indicated.) For example, select Go To Next Page.

5. A thick dashed bounding box and a button symbol in the bottom right corner indicate that an object is a button.

6. Use the Preview panel to preview and test the button. (See page 227 for further information.)

Hot tip

You can place navigation buttons such as next/previous page buttons on a master page so that you don't have to place the buttons repeatedly on individual document pages.

Beware

Some actions are specific to either SWF or PDF file formats and do not work for the other file format. For example, Go To Page is a SWF only action.

Hot tip

To create a rollover appearance for a button, move your cursor into the Appearance area of the Buttons panel. Click the [Rollover] state to make it active. Apply the change of appearance for the button object. For example, apply an Inner Glow effect to the button (see page 212–213 for information on applying Effects).

Media

You can add movie and sound clips to documents you intend to export as interactive PDF or SWF files. The Media panel allows you to import video and audio files and then control settings such as Poster Frame, Play on Page Load, Looping and specify a movie controller.

Hot tip

Recommended file formats you can import include Flash Video (.FLV and .FV4), H.264 (MP4) and .SWF. You can also import MP3 audio files. Older media types such as Quicktime (.MOV), .AVI and .WMV are still supported but do not have such complete and flexible support as provided by the more recent video and audio formats.

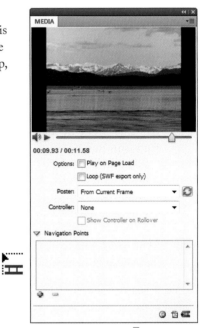

1. Placing movie or audio files is similar to placing images (see page 88). To add a movie clip, choose File>Place. Navigate to the file you want to place, click on it to select it, then click Open.

2. If a frame was active when you chose the File>Place command, the movie clip appears in the frame. If you did not have a selected frame you get the Loaded Media cursor. Either click or drag the Loaded Media cursor to place the video.

Beware

InDesign does not embed movie/audio files within the document; it links to media files in the same way that it links to images (see pages 93–94). If you transfer interactive documents to other users as part of your workflow, make sure you also send the original media files so that the links to them can be maintained.

3. A thumbnail preview of the video appears in the Media panel and a video symbol appears in the top left corner of the frame.

4. To set a poster frame – the image that appears in the movie frame to represent the movie before it is played – drag the movie scrubber below the movie thumbnail to select a frame, then click the Use Frame as Poster button ( ). The Poster pop-up menu allows you choose a different image if required.

5. Use the Controller pop-up menu to select the controller you want to make available to the user when they play the movie.

Hot tip

Click the Set Options for Interactive PDF button (🗂), at the bottom of the Media panel to access options for video presentation and playback in PDFs.

6. Click the Play/Pause button below the movie thumbnail to preview the movie in the Movie panel. Use the Preview panel to preview the movie with its movie controller and alongside other interactive elements on the page.

Multi-state object slide shows

The Object States panel allows you to create an object with multiple versions or states. Multi-state objects are commonly used to set up image slide shows, where different images form the multiple states, with previous and next buttons to allow the viewer to cycle through the states to view images in sequence.

1 To create a multi-state slide show, place images on a page that you want to include in the slide show. Slide shows work best if the image frame sizes are identical and if images are all portrait or all landscape orientation.

2 Use the Align panel, if necessary to ensure that image frames are positioned in a stack one on top of another. Make sure that all the image frames remain selected.

3 Show the Object States panel if it is not already visible.

4 Click the Convert Selection to Multi-State Object button (▣). Each individual image appears as a state in the Object States panel. You can drag individual states up or down to change the order in which they appear.

5 To indicate its status as a multi-state object, a thick, dashed boundary box appears around the object on the page, together with the multi-state icon in the bottom right corner.

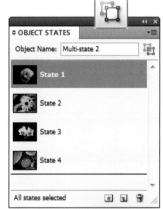

6 Create and position previous and next buttons that trigger Go To Previous/ Next State actions (see page 229 for information on creating buttons).

(see page 229 for information on creating buttons)

Hot tip

Create buttons to allow the user to cycle through images in the slide show. Set the action for forward and back buttons, in the Buttons panel, to Go To Next State/Go To Previous State respectively.

Beware

Go To Next State/Previous State actions are only available for export to SWF file format.

Hyperlinks

One of the most fundamental aspects of any interactive document is the inclusion of hyperlinks that allow interlinking of pages within a document and to a vast array of pages and other resources available on the web. Use the Hyperlinks panel to create hyperlinks in interactive documents.

1. To create hyperlinked text, start by highlighting the text you want to become the clickable hyperlink. This is referred to as the source text.

2. Show the Hyperlink panel. Click the Create New Hyperlink button ( ) at the bottom of the Hyperlinks panel.

4. Leave the Link to pop-up menu set to URL. Enter the destination url for the hyperlink in the URL entry box. Make sure you retain the http:// resource protocol. Deselect the Shared Hyperlink Destination checkbox.

5. If required, switch on the Character Style option then select a character style from the pop-up menu to apply character settings to control the appearance of hyperlinks. For example, the default appearance for hyperlinks on the web is blue and underlined.

6. Use Appearance options to indicate a hyperlink with a visible bounding box, to control the appearance of the bounding box and the highlight appearance of a hyperlink when the user clicks it.

7. To edit settings for a hyperlink click once on the hyperlink entry in the list box to select it; then choose Hyperlink Options from the Hyperlinks panel menu. Or, double-click the Hyperlink entry.

Export to SWF

A .SWF file is an interactive file that is finalized and ready to be placed in a Web page or for viewing on a device that supports Flash Player. SWF files can include animation, audio, video and remote rollover effects, as well as buttons, hyperlinks and page transitions.

1 When you are ready to export to SWF, choose File>Export. Select Flash Player (SWF) from the Save as type pop-up menu (Windows), Format pop-up (Mac). Click Save.

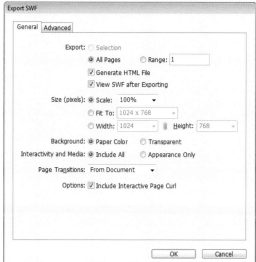

2 In the General tab of the Export SWF dialog box create the settings you require. Specify a page range for export if you don't want to export the entire document.

3 It is useful to keep Generate HTML file and View SWF after Exporting selected to quickly preview and test the interactive document in a browser as soon as you export it.

4 You can scale the size of the interactive document if required using percentage or pixel values.

5 Select Transparent to create a transparent background for your SWF. Page transitions and interactive page curl settings are disabled if you specify a transparent background.

6 You can override page transition settings in the InDesign document by selecting an option from the Page Transitions pop-up menu. Select the Interactive Page Curl checkbox if you want users to be able to drag corners to flip from page to page.

7 Click the Advanced tab to change default settings for type, images and Frame Rate.

Hot tip

Export to .FLA file format when you want to hand over the document to a Flash developer to add advanced interactive functions prior to exporting to SWF.

Hot tip

To create page transitions that export to SWF and Interactive PDF, select a page or range of pages in the Pages panel, then select a transition type from the Transitions pop-up menu in the Page Transitions panel.

Beware

If you select either the Rasterize Pages or the Flatten Transparency options in the Advanced tab, interactive features in the exported document are lost.

Export to Interactive PDF

An interactive PDF can contain interactive buttons, hyperlinks, movies, audio and page transitions. Dynamic PDFs are a good way to deliver interactive slide shows and presentations.

Beware

When you export an interactive PDF make sure you select Adobe PDF (Interactive) from the Save as type (Windows)/Format (Mac) pop-up menu.

 When you are ready to export your document as an Interactive PDF, choose File>Export. Select Adobe PDF (Interactive) from the Save as type pop-up (Windows), Format pop-up (Mac). Specify the location where you want to save the file, then click the Save button. Create settings for the interactive PDF as required.

| File name: | d_interactive.pdf |
| Save as type: | Adobe PDF (Interactive) |

2 Set a page range if you don't want to export the entire InDesign document.

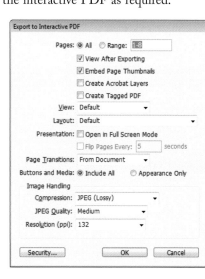

3 Select View After Exporting to launch Acrobat Reader automatically so that you can preview and test the PDF immediately.

Beware

Interactive PDFs do not support animations.

4 Use the View pop-up if you want to scale the PDF so that is displays larger or smaller than the original. The Layout pop-up allows you to create PDFs that display pages side by side as spreads.

5 Use the Page Transitions pop-up menu to specify a single transition type that will override any page transitions set up in the InDesign document.

6 For Buttons and Media, make sure you leave the Include All radio button selected. If you select Appearance Only interactive features do not export.

7 Create settings for Image Handling. A typical resolution used for web and multimedia content is 72ppi. The iPad uses a screen resolution of 132ppi. Increasing the resolution increases the file size.

Index

T